Wit and Wisdom of Don Quixote

Miguel de Cervantes Saavedra

Down in a village of La Mancha, the name of which I have no desire to recollect, there lived, not long ago, one of those gentlemen who usually keep a lance upon a rack, an old buckler, a lean horse, and a coursing grayhound. Soup, composed of somewhat more mutton than beef, the fragments served up cold on most nights, lentils on Fridays, collops and eggs on Saturdays, and a pigeon by way of addition on Sundays, consumed three-fourths of his income; the remainder of it supplied him with a cloak of fine cloth, velvet breeches, with slippers of the same for holidays, and a suit of the best homespun, in which he adorned himself on week-days. His family consisted of a housekeeper above forty, a niece not quite twenty, and a lad who served him both in the field and at home, who could saddle the horse or handle the pruning-hook. The age of our gentleman bordered upon fifty years: he was of a strong constitution, spare-bodied, of a meagre visage, a very early riser, and a lover of the chase. Some pretend to say that his surname was Quixada or Quesada, for on this point his historians differ; though, from very probable conjectures, we may conclude that his name was Quixana. This is, however, of little importance to our history; let it suffice that, in relating it, we do not swerve a jot from the truth.

In fine, his judgment being completely obscured, he was seized with one of the strangest fancies that ever entered the head of any madman; this was, a belief that it behooved him, as well for the advancement of his glory as the service of his country, to become a knight-errant, and traverse the world, armed and mounted, in quest of adventures, and to practice all that had been performed by knights-errant of whom he had read; redressing every species of grievance, and exposing himself to dangers, which, being surmounted, might secure to him eternal glory and renown. The poor gentleman imagined himself at least crowned Emperor of Trebisond, by the valor of his arm; and thus wrapped in these agreeable delusions and borne away by the extraordinary pleasure he found in them, he hastened to put his designs into execution.

The first thing he did was to scour up some rusty armor which had been his great-grandfather's, and had lain many years neglected in a corner. This he cleaned and adjusted as well as he could; but he found one grand defect,—the helmet was incomplete, having only the morion. This deficiency, however, he ingeniously supplied by making a kind of visor of pasteboard, which, being fixed to the morion, gave the appearance of an entire helmet. It is true, indeed, that, in order to prove its strength, he drew his sword, and gave it two strokes, the first of which instantly demolished the labor of a week; but not altogether approving of the facility with which it was destroyed, and in order to secure himself against a similar misfortune, he made another visor, which, having fenced in the inside with small bars of iron, he felt assured of its strength, and, without making any more experiments, held it to be a most excellent helmet.

In the next place he visited his steed; and although this animal had more blemishes than the horse of Gonela, which, "tantum pellis et ossa fuit," yet, in his eyes, neither the Bucephalus of Alexander nor the Cid's Babieca, could be compared with him. Four days was he deliberating upon what name he should give him; for, as he said to himself, it would be very improper that a horse so excellent, appertaining to a knight so famous, should be without an appropriate name; he therefore endeavored to find one that should express what he had been before he belonged to a knight-errant, and also what he now was: nothing could, indeed, be more reasonable than that, when the master changed his state, the horse should likewise change his name and assume one pompous and high-sounding, as became the new order he now professed. So, after having devised, altered, lengthened, curtailed, rejected, and again framed in his imagination a variety of names, he finally determined upon Rozinante, a name in his opinion lofty, sonorous, and full of meaning; importing that he had only been a rozin—a drudge horse—before his present condition, and that now he was before all the rozins in the world.

Having given his horse a name so much to his satisfaction, he resolved to fix upon one for himself. This consideration employed him eight more days, when at length he determined to call himself Don Quixote; whence some of the historians of this most true history have concluded that his name was certainly Quixada, and not Quesada, as others would have it. Then recollecting that the valorous Amadis, not content with the simple appellation of Amadis, added thereto the name of his kingdom and native country, in order to render it famous, styling himself Amadis de Gaul; so he, like a good knight, also added the name of his province, and called himself Don Quixote de la Mancha; whereby, in his opinion, he fully proclaimed his lineage and country, which, at the same time, he honored by taking its name.

His armor being now furbished, his helmet made perfect, his horse and himself provided with names, he found nothing wanting but a lady to be in love with, as he said,—

"A knight-errant without a mistress was a tree without either fruit or leaves, and a body without a soul!"

One morning before day, being one of the most sultry in the month of July, he armed himself cap-a-pie, mounted Rozinante, placed the helmet on his head, braced on his target, took his lance, and, through the private gate of his back yard, issued forth into the open plain, in a transport of joy to think he had met with no obstacles to the commencement of his honorable enterprise. But scarce had he found himself on the plain when he was assailed by a recollection so terrible as almost to make him abandon the undertaking; for it just then occurred to him that he was not yet dubbed a knight; therefore, in conformity to the laws of chivalry, he neither could nor ought to enter the lists against any of that order; and, if he had been actually dubbed he should, as a new knight, have worn white armor, without any device on his shield, until he had gained one by force of arms. These considerations made him irresolute whether to proceed, but frenzy prevailing over reason, he determined to get himself made a knight by the first one he should meet, like many others of whom he had read. As to white armor, he resolved, when he had an opportunity, to scour his own, so that it should be whiter than ermine. Having now composed his mind, he proceeded, taking whatever road his horse pleased; for therein, he believed, consisted the true spirit of adventure. Everything that our adventurer saw and conceived was, by his imagination, moulded to what he had read; so in his eyes the inn appeared to be a castle, with its four turrets, and pinnacles of shining silver, together with its drawbridge, deep moat, and all the appurtenances with which such castles are visually described. When he had advanced within a short distance of it, he checked Rozinante, expecting some dwarf would mount the battlements, to announce by sound of trumpet the arrival of a knight-errant at the castle; but, finding them tardy, and Rozinante impatient for the stable, he approached the inn-door, and there saw the two girls, who to him appeared to be beautiful damsels or lovely dames enjoying themselves before the gate of their castle.

It happened that, just at this time, a swineherd collecting his hogs (I make no apology, for so they are called) from an adjoining stubblefield, blew the horn which assembles them together, and instantly Don Quixote was satisfied, for he imagined it was a dwarf who had given the signal of his arrival. With extraordinary satisfaction, therefore, he went up to the inn; upon which the ladies, being startled at the sight of a man armed in that manner, with lance and buckler, were retreating into the house; but Don Quixote, perceiving their alarm, raised his pasteboard visor, thereby partly discovering his meagre, dusty visage, and with gentle demeanor and placid voice, thus addressed them: "Fly not, ladies, nor fear any discourtesy, for it would be wholly inconsistent with the order of knighthood, which I profess, to offer insult to any person, much less to virgins of that exalted rank which your appearance indicates." The girls stared at him, and were endeavoring to find out his face, which was almost concealed by the sorry visor; but hearing themselves called virgins, they could not forbear laughing, and to such a degree that Don Quixote was displeased, and said to them: "Modesty well becomes beauty, and excessive laughter proceeding from slight cause is folly."

This language, so unintelligible to the ladies, added to the uncouth figure of our knight, increased their laughter; consequently he grew more indignant, and would have proceeded further but for the timely appearance of the innkeeper, a very corpulent and therefore a very pacific man, who, upon seeing so ludicrous an object, armed, and with accoutrements so ill-sorted as were the bridle, lance, buckler, and corselet, felt disposed to join the damsels in demonstrations of mirth; but, in truth, apprehending some danger from a form thus strongly fortified, he resolved to behave with civility, and therefore said, "If, Sir Knight, you are seeking for a lodging, you will here find, excepting a bed (for there are none in this inn), everything in abundance." Don Quixote, perceiving the humility of the governor of the fortress,—for such to him appeared the innkeeper,—answered, "For me, Signor Castellano, anything will suffice, since arms are my ornaments, warfare my repose." The host thought he called him Castellano because he took him for a sound Castilian, whereas he was an Andalusian of the coast of St. Lucar, as great a thief as Cacus and not less mischievous than a collegian or a page; and he replied, "If so, your worship's beds must be hard rocks, and your sleep continual watching; and that being the case, you may dismount with a certainty of finding here sufficient cause for keeping awake the whole year, much more a single night." So saying, he laid hold of Don Quixote's stirrup, who alighted with much difficulty and pain, for he had fasted the whole of the day. He then desired the host to take especial care of his steed, for it was the finest creature ever fed; the innkeeper examined him, but thought him not so good by half as his master had represented him. Having led the horse to the stable he returned to receive the orders of his guest, whom the damsels, being now reconciled to him, were disarming; they had taken off the back and breast plates, but endeavored in vain to disengage the gorget, or take off the counterfeit beaver, which he had fastened with green ribbons in such a manner that they could not be untied, and he would upon no account allow them to be cut; therefore he remained all that night with his helmet on, the strangest and most ridiculous figure imaginable.

While these light girls, whom he still conceived to be persons of quality and ladies of the castle, were disarming him, he said to them, with infinite grace: "Never before was knight so honored by ladies as Don Quixote, after his departure from his native village! damsels attended upon him; princesses took charge of his steed! O Rosinante,—for that, ladies, is the name of my horse, and Don Quixote de la Mancha my own; although it was not my intention to have discovered myself until deeds performed in your service should have proclaimed me; but impelled to make so just an application of that ancient romance of Lanzarote to my present situation, I have thus prematurely disclosed my name: yet the time shall come when your ladyships may command, and I obey; when the valor of my arm shall make manifest the desire I have to serve you." The girls, unaccustomed to such rhetorical flourishes, made no reply, but asked whether he would please to eat anything. "I shall willingly take some food," answered Don Quixote, "for I apprehend it would be of much service to me." That day happened to be Friday, and there was nothing in the house but some fish of that kind which in Castile is called Abadexo; in Andalusia, Bacallao; in some parts, Curadillo: and in others, Truchuela. They asked if his worship would like some truchuela, for they had no other fish to offer him. "If there be many troutlings," replied Don Quixote, "they will supply the place of one trout; for it is the same to me whether I receive eight single rials or one piece-of-eight. Moreover, these troutlings may be preferable, as veal is better than beef, and kid superior to goat. Be that as it may, let it come immediately, for the toil and weight of arms cannot be sustained by the body unless the interior be supplied with aliments." For the benefit of the cool air, they placed the table at the door of the inn, and the landlord produced some of his ill-soaked and worse-cooked bacallao, with bread as foul and black as the knight's armor. But it was a spectacle highly risible to see him eat; for his hands being engaged in holding his helmet on and raising the beaver, he could not feed himself, therefore one of the ladies performed that office for him; but to drink would have been utterly impossible had not the innkeeper bored a reed, and placing one end into his mouth at the other poured in the wine; and all this he patiently endured rather than cut the lacings of his helmet.

THE PLEASANT METHOD DON QUIXOTE TOOK TO BE DUBBED A KNIGHT.

It troubled him to reflect that he was not yet a knight, feeling persuaded that he could not lawfully engage in any adventure until he had been invested with the order of knighthood.

Agitated by this idea, he abruptly finished his scanty supper, called the innkeeper, and, shutting himself up with him in the stable, he fell on his knees before him and said, "Never will I arise from this place, valorous knight, until your courtesy shall vouchsafe to grant a boon which it is my intention to request,—a boon that will redound to your glory and to the benefit of all mankind." The innkeeper, seeing his guest at his feet and hearing such language, stood confounded and stared at him without knowing what to do or say; he entreated him to rise, but in vain, until he had promised to grant the boon he requested. "I expected no less, signor, from your great magnificence," replied Don Quixote; "know, therefore, that the boon I have demanded, and which your liberality has conceded, is that on the morrow you will confer upon me the honor of knighthood. This night I will watch my arms in the chapel of your castle, in order that, in the morning, my earnest desire may be fulfilled and I may with propriety traverse the four quarters of the world in quest of adventures for the relief of the distressed, conformable to the duties of chivalry and of knights-errant, who, like myself, are devoted to such pursuits."

The host, who, as we have said, was a shrewd fellow, and had already entertained some doubts respecting the wits of his guest, was now confirmed in his suspicions; and to make sport for the night, determined to follow his humor. He told him, therefore, that his desire was very reasonable, and that such pursuits were natural and suitable to knights so illustrious as he appeared to be, and as his gallant demeanor fully testified; that he had himself in the days of his youth followed that honorable profession, and travelled over various parts of the world in search of adventures; failing not to visit the suburbs of Malaga, the isles of Riaran, the compass of Seville, the market-place of Segovia, the olive-field of Valencia, the rondilla of Grenada, the coast of St. Lucar, the fountain of Cordova, the taverns of Toledo, and divers other parts, where he had exercised the agility of his heels and the dexterity of his hands; committing sundry wrongs, soliciting widows, seducing damsels, cheating youths,—in short, making himself known to most of the tribunals in Spain; and that, finally, he had retired to this castle, where he lived upon his revenue and that of others, entertaining therein all knights-errant of every quality and degree solely for the great affection he bore them, and that they might share their fortune with him in return for his good will. He further told him that in his castle there was no chapel wherein he could watch his armor, for it had been pulled down in order to be rebuilt; but that, in cases of necessity, he knew it might be done wherever he pleased. Therefore, he might watch it that night in a court of the castle, and the following morning, if it pleased God, the requisite ceremonies should be performed, and he should be dubbed so effectually that the world would not be able to produce a more perfect knight. He then inquired if he had any money about him. Don Quixote told him he had none, having never read in their histories that knights-errant provided themselves with money. The innkeeper assured him he was mistaken; for, admitting that it was not mentioned in their history, the authors deeming it unnecessary to specify things so obviously requisite as money and clean shirts, yet was it not therefore to be inferred that they had none; but, on the contrary, he might consider it as an established fact that all knights-errant, of whose histories so many volumes are filled, carried their purses well provided against accidents; that they were also supplied with shirts, and a small casket of ointments to heal the wounds they might receive, for in plains and deserts, where they fought and were wounded, no aid was near unless they had some sage enchanter for their friend, who could give them immediate assistance by conveying in cloud through the air some damsel or dwarf, with a phial of water possessed of such virtue that, upon tasting a single drop of it, they should instantly become as sound as if they had received no injury. But when the knights of former times were without such a friend, they always took care that their esquires should be provided with money and such necessary articles as lint and salves; and when they had no esquires—which very rarely happened—they carried these things themselves upon the crupper of their horse, in wallets so small as to be scarcely visible, that they might seem to be something of more importance; for, except in such cases, the custom of carrying wallets was not tolerated among knights-errant. He therefore advised, though, as his godson (which he was soon to be), he might command him, never henceforth to travel without money and the aforesaid provisions, and he would find them serviceable when he least expected it. Don Quixote promised to follow his advice with punctuality: and an order was now given for performing the watch of the armor in a large yard adjoining the inn. Don Quixote, having collected it together placed it on a cistern which was close to a well; then, bracing on his target and grasping his lance, with graceful demeanor he paced to and fro before the pile, beginning his parade as soon as it was dark.

The innkeeper informed all who were in the inn of the frenzy of his guest, the watching of his armor, and of the intended knighting.

The host repeated to him that there was no chapel in the castle, nor was it by any means necessary for what remained to be done; that the stroke of knighting consisted in blows on the neck and shoulders, according to the ceremonial of the order, which might be effectually performed in the middle of the field; that the duty of watching his armor he had now completely fulfilled, for he had watched more than four hours, though only two were required. All this Don Quixote believed, and said that he was there ready to obey him, requesting him, at the same time, to perform the deed as soon as possible; because, should he be assaulted again when he found himself knighted, he was resolved not to leave one person alive in the castle, excepting those whom, out of respect to him, and at his particular request, he might be induced to spare. The constable, thus warned and alarmed, immediately brought forth a book in which he kept his account of the straw and oats he furnished to the carriers, and attended by a boy, who carried an end of candle, and the two damsels before mentioned, went towards Don Quixote, whom he commanded to kneel down; he then began reading in his manual, as if it were some devout prayer, in the course of which he raised his hand and gave him a good blow on the neck, and, after that, a handsome stroke over the shoulders, with his own sword, still muttering between his teeth, as if in prayer. This being done, he commanded one of the ladies to gird on his sword, an office she performed with much alacrity, as well as discretion, no small portion of which was necessary to avoid bursting with laughter at every part of the ceremony; but indeed the prowess they had seen displayed by the new knight kept their mirth within bounds.

At girding on the sword, the good lady said: "God grant you may be a fortunate knight and successful in battle."

Don Quixote inquired her name, that he might thenceforward know to whom he was indebted for the favor received, as it was his intention to bestow upon her some share of the honor he should acquire by the valor of his arm. She replied, with much humility, that her name was Tolosa, and that she was the daughter of a cobbler at Toledo, who lived at the stalls of Sanchobienaya; and that, wherever she was, she would serve and honor him as her lord. Don Quixote, in reply, requested her, for his sake, to do him the favor henceforth to add to her name the title of don, and call herself Donna Tolosa, which she promised to do. The other girl now buckled on his spur, and with her he held nearly the same conference as with the lady of the sword; having inquired her name, she told him it was Molinera, and that she was daughter to an honest miller of Antiquera: he then requested her likewise to assume the don, and style herself Donna Molinera, renewing his proffers of service and thanks.

These never-till-then-seen ceremonies being thus speedily performed, Don Quixote was impatient to find himself on horseback, in quest of adventures. He therefore instantly saddled Rozinante, mounted him, and, embracing his host, made his acknowledgments for the favor he had conferred by knighting him, in terms so extraordinary, that it would be in vain to attempt to repeat them. The host, in order to get rid of him the sooner, replied, with no less flourish, but more brevity; and, without making any demand for his lodging, wished him a good journey.

The tongue slow and the eyes quick.

Keep your mouth shut and your eyes open.

The brave man carves out his own fortune.

Very full of pain, yet soon as he was able to stir, he began to roll himself on the ground, and to repeat, in what they affirm was said by the wounded knight of the wood:—

"Where art thou, mistress of my heart,

Unconscious of thy lover's smart?

Ah me! thou know'st not my distress,

Or thou art false and pitiless."

"I know who I am," answered Don Quixote; "and I know, too, that I am not only capable of being those I have mentioned, but all the twelve peers of France, yea, and the nine worthies, since my exploits will far exceed all that they have jointly or separately achieved."

DESTRUCTION OF DON QUIXOTE'S LIBRARY

Long and heavy was the sleep of Don Quixote: meanwhile the priest having asked the niece for the key of the chamber containing the books, those authors of the mischief, which she delivered with a very good will, they entered, attended by the housekeeper, and found above a hundred large volumes well bound, besides a great number of smaller size. No sooner did the housekeeper see them than she ran out of the room in great haste, and immediately returned with a pot of holy water and a bunch of hyssop, saying: "Signor Licentiate, take this and sprinkle the room, lest some enchanter of the many that these books abound with should enchant us, as a punishment for our intention to banish them out of the world."

The priest smiled at the housekeeper's simplicity, and ordered the barber to reach him the books one by one, that they might see what they treated of, as they might perhaps find some that deserved not to be chastised by fire.

"No," said the niece, "there is no reason why any of them should be spared, for they have all been mischief-makers: so let them all be thrown out of the window into the courtyard; and having made a pile of them, set fire to it; or else make a bonfire of them in the back yard, where the smoke will offend nobody."

The housekeeper said the same, so eagerly did they both thirst for the death of those innocents. But the priest would not consent to it without first reading the titles at least.

The first that Master Nicholas put into his hands was "Amadis de Gaul," in four parts; and the priest said: "There seems to be some mystery in this, for I have heard say that this was the first book of chivalry printed in Spain, and that all the rest had their foundation and rise from it; I think, therefore, as head of so pernicious a sect, we ought to condemn him to the fire without mercy."

"Not so," said the barber; "for I have heard also that it is the best of all the books of this kind: therefore, as being unequalled in its way, it ought to be spared."

"You are right," said the priest, "and for that reason its life is granted for the present. Let us see that other next to him."

"It is," said the barber, "the 'Adventures of Esplandian,' the legitimate son of 'Amadis de Gaul.'"

"Verily," said the priest, "the goodness of the father shall avail the son nothing; take him, Mistress Housekeeper; open that casement, and throw him into the yard, and let him make a beginning to the pile for the intended bonfire."

The housekeeper did so with much satisfaction, and good Esplandian was sent flying into the yard, there to wait with patience for the fire with which he was threatened.

"Proceed," said the priest.

"The next," said the barber, "is 'Amadis of Greece;' yea, and all these on this side, I believe, are of the lineage of Amadis."

"Then into the yard with them all!" quoth the priest; "for rather than not burn Queen Pintiquiniestra, and the shepherd Darinel with his eclogues, and the devilish perplexities of the author, I would burn the father who begot me, were I to meet him in the shape of a knight-errant."

"Of the same opinion am I," said the barber.

"And I too," added the niece.

"Well, then," said the housekeeper, "away with them all into the yard." They handed them to her; and, as they were numerous, to save herself the trouble of the stairs, she threw them all out of the window.

"What tun of an author is that?" said the priest.

"This," answered the barber, "is 'Don Olivante de Laura.'"

"The author of that book," said the priest, "was the same who composed the 'Garden of Flowers;' and in good truth I know not which of the two books is the truest, or rather, the least lying: I can only say that this goes to the yard for its arrogance and absurdity."

"This that follows is 'Florismarte of Hyrcania,'" said the barber.

"What! is Signor Florismarte there?" replied the priest; "now, by my faith, he shall soon make his appearance in the yard, notwithstanding his strange birth and chimerical adventures; for the harshness and dryness of his style will admit of no excuse. To the yard with him, and this other, Mistress Housekeeper."

"With all my heart, dear sir," answered she, and with much joy executed what she was commanded.

"Here is the 'Knight Platir,'" said the barber.

"That," said the priest, "is an ancient book, and I find nothing in him deserving pardon: without more words, let him be sent after the rest;" which was accordingly done. They opened another book, and found it entitled the "Knight of the Cross." "So religious a title," quoth the priest, "might, one would think, atone for the ignorance of the author; but it is a common saying 'the devil lurks behind the cross:' so to the fire with him."

The barber, taking down another book, said, "This is 'The Mirror of Chivalry.'"

"Oh! I know his worship very well," quoth the priest. "I am only for condemning this to perpetual banishment because it contains some things of the famous Mateo Boyardo.

"If I find him here uttering any other language than his own, I will show no respect; but if he speaks in his own tongue, I will put him upon my head."

"I have him in Italian," said the barber, "but I do not understand him."

"Neither is it any great matter, whether you understand him or not," answered the priest; "and we would willingly have excused the good captain from bringing him into Spain and making him a Castilian; for he has deprived him of a great deal of his native value; which, indeed, is the misfortune of all those who undertake the translation of poetry into other languages; for, with all their care and skill, they can never bring them on a level with the original production. This book, neighbor, is estimable upon two accounts; the one, that it is very good of itself; and the other, because there is a tradition that it was written by an ingenious king of Portugal. All the adventures of the castle of Miraguarda are excellent, and contrived with much art; the dialogue courtly and clear; and all the characters preserved with great judgment and propriety. Therefore, Master Nicholas, saving your better judgment, let this and 'Amadis de Gaul' be exempted from the fire, and let all the rest perish without any further inquiry."

"Not so, friend," replied the barber; "for this which I have here is the renowned 'Don Bellianis.'"

The priest replied: "This, and the second, third, and fourth parts, want a little rhubarb to purge away their excess of bile; besides, we must remove all that relates to the castle of Fame, and other absurdities of greater consequence; for which let sentence of transportation be passed upon them, and, according as they show signs of amendment, they shall be treated with mercy or justice. In the mean time, neighbor, give them room in your house; but let them not be read."

"With all my heart," quoth the barber; and without tiring himself any farther in turning over books of chivalry, bid the housekeeper take all the great ones and throw them into the yard. This was not spoken to the stupid or deaf, but to one who had a greater mind to be burning them than weaving the finest and largest web; and therefore, laying hold of seven or eight at once, she tossed them out at the window.

But, in taking so many together, one fell at the barber's feet, who had a mind to see what it was, and found it to be the history of the renowned knight Tirante the White. "Heaven save me!" quoth the priest, with a loud voice, "is Tirante the White there? Give him to me, neighbor; for in him I shall have a treasure of delight, and a mine of entertainment. Here we have Don Kyrie-Eleison of Montalvan, a valorous knight, and his brother Thomas of Montalvan, with the knight Fonseca, and the combat which the valiant Tirante fought with the bull-dog, and the witticisms of the damsel Plazerdemivida; also the amours and artifices of the widow Reposada; and madam the Empress in love with her squire Hypolito. Verily, neighbor, in its way it is the best book in the world: here the knights eat and sleep, and die in their beds, and make their wills before their deaths; with several things which are not to be found in any other books of this kind. Notwithstanding this I tell you, the author deserved, for writing so many foolish things seriously, to be sent to the galleys for the whole of his life: carry it home, and read it, and you will find all I say of him to be true."

"I will do so," answered the barber: "but what shall we do with these small volumes that remain?"

"Those," said the priest, "are, probably, not books of chivalry, but of poetry." Then opening one he found it was the 'Diana' of George de Montemayor, and, concluding that all the others were of the same kind, he said, "These do not deserve to be burnt like the rest; for they cannot do the mischief that those of chivalry have done; they are works of genius and fancy, and do injury to none."

"O sir," said the niece, "pray order them to be burnt with the rest; for should my uncle be cured of this distemper of chivalry, he may possibly, by reading such books, take it into his head to turn shepherd, and wander through the woods and fields, singing and playing on a pipe; and what would be still worse, turn poet, which, they say, is an incurable and contagious disease."

"The damsel says true," quoth the priest, "and it will not be amiss to remove this stumbling-block out of our friend's way. And, since we begin with the 'Diana' of Montemayor, my opinion is that it should not be burnt, but that all that part should be expunged which treats of the sage Felicia, and of the enchanted fountain, and also most of the longer poems; leaving him, in God's name, the prose and also the honor of being the first in that kind of writing."

"The next that appears," said the barber, "is the Diana, called the second, by Salmantino; and another, of the same name, whose author is Gil Polo."

"The Salmantinian," answered the priest, "may accompany and increase the number of the condemned—to the yard with him: but let that of Gil Polo be preserved, as if it were written by Apollo himself. Proceed, friend, and let us despatch; for it grows late."

"This," said the barber, opening another, "is the 'Ten Books of the Fortune of Love,' composed by Antonio de lo Frasso, a Sardinian poet."

"By the holy orders I have received!" said the priest, "since Apollo was Apollo, the muses muses, and the poets poets, so humorous and so whimsical a book as this was never written; it is the best, and most extraordinary of the kind that ever appeared in the world; and he who has not read it may be assured that he has never read anything of taste: give it me here, neighbor, for I am better pleased at finding it than if I had been presented with a cassock of Florence satin." He laid it aside, with great satisfaction, and the barber proceeded, saying:—

"These which follow are the 'Shepherd of Iberia,' the 'Nymphs of Enares,' and the 'Cure of Jealousy.'"

"Then you have only to deliver them up to the secular arm of the housekeeper," said the priest, "and ask me not why, for in that case we should never have done."

"The next is the 'Shepherd of Filida.'"

"He is no shepherd," said the priest, "but an ingenious courtier; let him be preserved, and laid up as a precious jewel."

"This bulky volume here," said the barber, "is entitled the 'Treasure of Divers Poems.'"

"Had they been fewer," replied the priest, "they would have been more esteemed: it is necessary that this book should be weeded and cleared of some low things interspersed amongst its sublimities: let it be preserved, both because the author is my friend, and out of respect to other more heroic and exalted productions of his pen."

"This," pursued the barber, "is 'El Cancionero' of Lopez Maldonado."

"The author of that book," replied the priest, "is also a great friend of mine: his verses, when sung by himself, excite much admiration; indeed such is the sweetness of his voice in singing them, that they are perfectly enchanting. He is a little too prolix in his eclogues; but there can never be too much of what is really good: let it be preserved with the select. But what book is that next to it?"

"The 'Galatea' of Miguel de Cervantes," said the barber.

"That Cervantes has been an intimate friend of mine these many years, and I know that he is more versed in misfortunes than in poetry. There is a good vein of invention in his book, which proposes something, though nothing is concluded. We must wait for the second part, which he has promised: perhaps, on his amendment, he may obtain that entire pardon which is now denied him; in the mean time, neighbor, keep him a recluse in your chamber."

"With all my heart," answered the barber. "Now, here come three together: the 'Araucana' of Don Alonzo de Ercilla, the 'Austriada' of Juan Rufo, a magistrate of Cordova, and the 'Monserrato' of Christoval de Virves, a poet of Valencia."

"These three books," said the priest, "are the best that are written in heroic verse in the Castilian tongue, and may stand in competition with the most renowned works of Italy. Let them be preserved as the best productions of the Spanish Muse."

The priest grew tired of looking over so many books, and therefore, without examination, proposed that all the rest should be burnt; but the barber, having already opened one called the "Tears of Angelica," "I should have shed tears myself," said the priest, on hearing the name, "had I ordered that book to be burnt; for its author was one of the most celebrated poets, not only of Spain, but of the whole world: his translations from Ovid are admirable."

The same night the housekeeper set fire to and burnt all the books that were in the yard and in the house. Some must have perished that deserved to be treasured up in perpetual archives, but their destiny or the indolence of the scrutineer forbade it; and in them was fulfilled the saying, that—

"The just sometimes suffer for the unjust."

In the mean time Don Quixote tampered with a laborer, a neighbor of his, and an honest man (if such an epithet can be given to one that is poor), but shallow brained; in short, he said so much, used so many arguments, and made so many promises, that the poor fellow resolved to sally out with him and serve him in the capacity of a squire. Among other things, Don Quixote told him that he ought to be very glad to accompany him, for such an adventure might some time or the other occur, that by one stroke an island might be won, where he might leave him governor. With this and other promises, Sancho Panza (for that was the laborer's name) left his wife and children and engaged himself as squire to his neighbor.

Sancho Panza proceeded upon his ass, like a patriarch, with his wallet and leathern bottle, and with a vehement desire to find himself governor of the island, which his master had promised him. Don Quixote happened to take the same route as on his first expedition, over the plain of Montiel, which he passed with less inconvenience than before, for it was early in the morning, and the rays of the sun, darting on them horizontally, did not annoy them. Sancho Panza now said to his master: "I beseech your worship, good sir knight-errant, not to forget your promise concerning that same island; for I shall know how to govern it, be it ever so large."

To which Don Quixote answered: "Thou must know, friend Sancho Panza, that it was a custom much in use among the knights-errant of old to make their squires governors of the islands or kingdoms they conquered, and I am determined that so laudable a custom, shall not be lost through my neglect; on the contrary, I resolve to outdo them in it: for they sometimes, and perhaps most times, waited till their squires were grown old; and when they were worn out in their service, and had endured many bad days and worse nights, they conferred on them some title, such as count, or at least marquis, of some valley or province of more or less account; but if you live, and I live, before six days have passed I may probably win such a kingdom as may have others depending on it, just fit for thee to be crowned king of one of them. And do not think this any extraordinary matter, for things fall out to knights by such unforeseen and unexpected ways, that I may easily give thee more than I promise."

"So then," answered Sancho Panza, "if I were a king by some of those miracles your worship mentions, Joan Gutierrez, my duck, would come to be a queen, and my children infantas!"

"Who doubts it?" answered Don Quixote.

"I doubt it," replied Sancho Panza, "for I am verily persuaded that, if God were to rain down kingdoms upon the earth, none of them would sit well upon the head of Mary Gutierrez; for you must know, sir, she is not worth two farthings for a queen. The title of countess would sit better upon her, with the help of Heaven and good friends."

"Recommend her to God, Sancho," answered Don Quixote, "and he will do what is best for her, but do thou have a care not to debase thy mind so low as to content thyself with being less than a viceroy."

"Heaven grant us good success, and that we may speedily get this island which costs me so dear. No matter then how soon I die."

"I have already told thee, Sancho, to give thyself no concern upon that account; for, if an island cannot be had, there is the kingdom of Denmark or that of Sobradisa, which will fit thee like a ring to the finger. Besides, as they are upon terra firma, thou shouldst prefer them. But let us leave this to its own time, and see if thou hast anything for us to eat in thy wallet. We will then go in quest of some castle, where we may lodge this night and make the balsam that I told thee of, for I declare that my ear pains me exceedingly."

"I have here an onion and a piece of cheese, and I know not how many crusts of bread," said Sancho, "but they are not eatables fit for so valiant a knight as your worship."

"How little dost thou understand of this matter!" answered Don Quixote. "I tell thee, Sancho, that it is honorable in knights-errant not to eat once in a month; and, if they do taste food, it must be what first offers: and this thou wouldst have known hadst thou read as many histories as I have done; for, though I have perused many, I never yet found in them any account of knights-errant taking food, unless it were by chance and at certain sumptuous banquets prepared expressly for them. The rest of their days they lived, as it were, upon smelling. And though it is to be presumed they could not subsist without eating and satisfying all other wants,—as, in fact, they were men,—yet, since they passed most part of their lives in wandering through forests and deserts, and without a cook, their usual diet must have consisted of rustic viands, such as those which thou hast now offered me. Therefore, friend Sancho, let not that trouble thee which gives me pleasure, nor endeavor to make a new world, or to throw knight-errantry off its hinges."

"Pardon me, sir," said Sancho; "for, as I can neither read nor write, as I told you before, I am entirely unacquainted with the rules of the knightly profession; but henceforward I will furnish my wallet with all sorts of dried fruits for your worship, who are a knight; and for myself, who am none, I will supply it with poultry and other things of more substance."

There cannot be too much of a good thing.

What is lost to-day may be won to-morrow.

A saint may sometimes suffer for a sinner.

Many go out for wool and return shorn.

Matters of war are most subject to continual change.

Every man that is aggrieved is allowed to defend himself by all laws human and divine.

Truth is the mother of history, the rival of time, the depository of great actions, witness of the past, example and adviser of the present, and oracle of future ages.

Love, like knight-errantry, puts all things on a level.

He that humbleth himself God will exalt.

After Don Quixote had satisfied his hunger, he took up a handful of acorns, and, looking on them attentively, gave utterance to expressions like these:—

"Happy times and happy ages were those which the ancients termed the Golden Age! Not because gold, so prized in this our Iron age, was to be obtained, in that fortunate period, without toil; but because they who then lived were ignorant of those two words, Mine and Thine. In that blessed age all things were in common; to provide their ordinary sustenance no other labor was necessary than to raise their hands and take it from the sturdy oaks, which stood liberally inviting them to taste their sweet and relishing fruit. The limpid fountains and running streams offered them, in magnificent abundance, their delicious and transparent waters. In the clefts of rocks, and in hollow trees, the industrious and provident bees formed their commonwealths, offering to every hand, without interest, the fertile produce of their most delicious toil. The stately cork-trees, impelled by their own courtesy alone, divested themselves of their light and expanded bark, with which men began to cover their houses, supported by rough poles, only as a defence against the inclemency of the heavens. All then was peace, all amity, all concord. The heavy colter of the crooked plough had not yet dared to force open and search into the tender bowels of our first mother, who, unconstrained, offered from every part of her fertile and spacious bosom whatever might feed, sustain, and delight those, her children, by whom she was then possessed."

ANTONIO

Yes, lovely nymph, thou art my prize;
I boast the conquest of thy heart,
Though nor the tongue, nor speaking eyes,
Have yet revealed the latent smart.
Thy wit and sense assure my fate,
In them my love's success I see;
Nor can he be unfortunate
Who dares avow his flame for thee.

Yet sometimes hast thou frowned, alas!
And given my hopes a cruel shock;
Then did thy soul seem formed of brass,
Thy snowy bosom of the rock.
But in the midst of thy disdain,
Thy sharp reproaches, cold delays,

Hope from behind to ease my pain,
The border of her robe displays.
Ah, lovely maid! in equal scale
Weigh well thy shepherd's truth and love,
Which ne'er but with his breath can fail,
Which neither frowns nor smiles can move.
If love, as shepherds wont to say,
Be gentleness and courtesy,
So courteous is Olalia,
My passion will rewarded be.
And if obsequious duty paid,
The grateful heart can never move,
Mine sure, my fair, may well persuade
A due return and claim thy love.
For, to seem pleasing in thy sight,
I dress myself with studious care,
And, in my best apparel dight,
My Sunday clothes on Monday wear.
And shepherds say I'm not to blame,
For cleanly dress and spruce attire

Preserve alive love's wanton flame
And gently fan the dying fire.
To please my fair, in mazy ring
I join the dance, and sportive play;
And oft beneath thy window sing,
When first the cock proclaims the day.
With rapture on each charm I dwell,
And daily spread thy beauty's fame;
And still my tongue thy praise shall tell,

Though envy swell, or malice blame.

Teresa of the Berrocal,

When once I praised you, said in spite,

Your mistress you an angel call,

But a mere ape is your delight.

Thanks to the bugle's artful glare,

And all the graces counterfeit;

Thanks to the false and curléd hair,

Which wary Love himself might cheat.

I swore 'twas false, and said she lied;

At that her anger fiercely rose;

I boxed the clown that took her side,

And how I boxed my fairest knows.

I court thee not, Olalia,

To gratify a loose desire;

My love is chaste, without alloy

Of wanton wish or lustful fire.

The church hath silken cords, that tie

Consenting hearts in mutual bands:

If thou, my fair, its yoke will try,

Thy swain its ready captive stands.

If not, by all the saints I swear

On these bleak mountains still to dwell,

Nor ever quit my toilsome care,

But for the cloister and the cell.

I think I see her now, with that goodly presence, looking as if she had the sun on one side of her and the moon on the other; and above all, she was a notable housewife, and a friend to the poor; for which I believe her soul is at this very moment in heaven.

A clergyman must be over and above good, who makes all his parishioners speak well of him.

Parents ought not to settle their children against their will.

Though she does not fly or shun the company and conversation of the shepherds, but treats them in a courteous and friendly manner, yet, when any one of them ventures to discover his intention, though it be as just and holy as that of marriage, she casts him from her as out of a stone-bow. And by this sort of behavior she does more mischief in this country than if she carried the plague about with her; for her affability and beauty win the hearts of those who converse with her, and incline them to serve and love her; but her disdain and frank dealing drive them to despair; and so they know not what to say to her, and can only exclaim against her, calling her cruel and ungrateful, with such other titles as plainly denote her character; and, were you to abide here, sir, awhile, you would hear these mountains and valleys resound with the complaints of those rejected wretches that yet follow her. There is a place not far hence, where about two dozen of tall beeches grow, and not one of them is without the name of Marcela written and engraved on its smooth bark; over some of them is carved a crown, as if the lover would more clearly observe that Marcela deserves and wears the crown of all human beauty.

Revels, banquets, and repose, were invented for effeminate courtiers; but toil, disquietude, and arms alone were designed for those whom the world calls knights-errant.

For never sure was any knight

So served by damsel, or by dame,

As Lancelot, that man of might,

When he at first from Britain came.

The soldier who executes his captain's command is no less valuable than the captain who gave the order.

"I am of the same opinion," replied the traveller; "but one thing, among many others which appear to me to be censurable in knights-errant, is that, when they are prepared to engage in some great and perilous adventure to the manifest hazard of their lives, at the moment of attack they never think of commending themselves to God, as every Christian is bound to do at such a crisis, but rather commend themselves to their mistresses, and that with as much fervor and devotion as if they were really their God; a thing which to me savors of paganism."

"Signor," answered Don Quixote, "this can by no means be otherwise; and the knight-errant who should act in any other manner would digress much from his duty; for it is a received maxim and custom in chivalry, that the knight-errant, who, on the point of engaging in some great feat of arms, has his lady before him, must turn his eyes fondly and amorously towards her, as if imploring her favor and protection in the hazardous enterprise that awaits him; and, even if nobody hear him, he must pronounce some words between his teeth, by which he commends himself to her with his whole heart; and of this we have innumerable examples in history. Nor is it thence to be inferred that they neglect commending themselves to God; for there is time and opportunity enough to do it in the course of the action."

"Notwithstanding all that," replied the traveller, "better had it been if the words he spent in commending himself to his lady, in the midst of the career, had been employed as the duties of a Christian require; particularly as I imagine that all knights-errant have not ladies to commend themselves to, because they are not all in love."

"That cannot be," answered Don Quixote: "I say there cannot be a knight-errant without a mistress; for it is as essential and as natural for them to be enamored as for the sky to have stars; and most certainly, no history exists in which a knight-errant is to be found without an amour; for, from the very circumstance of his being without, he would not be acknowledged as a legitimate knight, but a bastard who had entered the fortress of chivalry, not by the gate, but over the pales, like a thief and robber."

"Nevertheless," said the traveller, "if I am not mistaken, I remember having read that Don Galaor, brother to the valorous Amadis de Gaul, never had a particular mistress, to whom he might commend himself; notwithstanding which, he was no less esteemed, and was a very valiant and famous knight."

To which our Don Quixote answered: "Signor, one swallow does not make a summer."

"If it is essential that every knight-errant be a lover," said the traveller, "it may well be presumed that you are yourself one, being of the profession; and, if you do not pique yourself upon the same secrecy as Don Galaor, I earnestly entreat you, in the name of all this good company and in my own, to tell us the name, country, quality, and beauty of your mistress, who cannot but account herself happy that all the world should know that she is loved and served by so worthy a knight."

Here Don Quixote breathed a deep sigh, and said: "I cannot positively affirm whether that sweet enemy of mine is pleased or not that the world should know I am her servant. I can only say, in answer to what you so very courteously inquire of me, that her name is Dulcinea; her country Toboso, a town of la Mancha: her quality at least that of a princess, since she is my queen and sovereign lady; her beauty more than human, since in her all the impossible and chimerical attributes of beauty which the poets ascribe to their mistresses are realized; for her hair is gold, her forehead the Elysian Fields, her eyebrows rainbows, her eyes suns, her cheeks roses, her lips coral, her teeth pearls, her neck, alabaster, her bosom marble, her hands ivory, her whiteness snow, and her whole person without parallel. She is of those of Toboso de la Mancha; a lineage which, though modern, is yet such as may give a noble beginning to the most illustrious families of future ages; and in this let no one contradict me, unless it be on the conditions that Zerbino fixed under the arms of Orlando, where it said:—

'That knight alone these arms shall move,

Who dares Orlando's prowess prove.'"

THE STORY OF CHRYSOSTOM

"Comrades," said he, "do you know what is passing in the village?"

"How should we know?" answered one of them.

"Know, then," continued the youth, "that the famous shepherd and scholar, Chrysostom, died this morning; and it is rumored that it was for love of that saucy girl Marcela, daughter of William the rich; she who rambles about these woods and fields in the dress of a shepherdess."

"For Marcela, say you?" quoth one.

"For her, I say," answered the goatherd; "and the best of it is, he has ordered in his will that they should bury him in the fields, like a Moor, at the foot of the rock, by the cork-tree fountain, which, according to report, and as they say, he himself declared was the very place where he first saw her. He ordered also other tilings so extravagant that the clergy say they must not be performed; nor is it fit that they should, for they seem to be heathenish. But his great friend Ambrosio, the student, who accompanied him, dressed also like a shepherd, declares that the whole of what Chrysostom enjoined shall be executed: and upon this the village is all in an uproar: but by what I can learn, they will at last do what Ambrosio and all his friends require; and to-morrow they come to inter him, with great solemnity, in the place I mentioned; and, in my opinion, it will be a sight well worth seeing; at least, I shall not fail to go, although I were certain of not returning to-morrow to the village."

"We will do the same," answered the goatherds; "and let us cast lots who shall stay behind to look after the goats."

"You say well, Pedro," quoth another; "but it will be needless to make use of this expedient, for I will remain for you all: and do not attribute this to self-denial or want of curiosity in me, but to the thorn which stuck into my foot the other day, and hinders me from walking."

"We thank you, nevertheless," answered Pedro.

Don Quixote requested Pedro to give him some account of the deceased man and the shepherdess. To which Pedro answered, "that all he knew was, that the deceased was a wealthy gentleman, and inhabitant of a village situate among these mountains, who had studied many years at Salamanca; at the end of which time he returned home, with the character of a very learned and well read person; particularly, it was said, he understood the science of the stars, and what the sun and moon are doing in the sky; for he told us punctually the clipse of the sun and moon."

"Friend," quoth Don Quixote, "the obscuration of those two luminaries is called an eclipse, and not a clipse."

But Pedro, not regarding niceties, went on with his story, saying, "He also foretold when the year would be plentiful or starel."

"Sterile, you would say, friend," quoth Don Quixote.

"Sterile, or starel," answered Pedro, "comes all to the same thing. And, as I was saying, his father and friends, who gave credit to his words, became very rich thereby; for they followed his advice in everything. This year he would say, 'Sow barley, and not wheat; in this you may sow vetches, and not barley; the next year there will be plenty of oil; the three following there will not be a drop.'"

"This science they call astrology," said Don Quixote.

"I know not how it is called," replied Pedro, "but I know that he knew all this, and more too. In short, not many months after he came from Salamanca, on a certain day he appeared dressed like a shepherd, with his crook and sheepskin jacket, having thrown aside his scholar's gown; and with an intimate friend of his, called Ambrosio, who had been his fellow-student, and who now put on likewise the apparel of a shepherd. I forgot to tell you how the deceased Chrysostom was a great man at making verses; insomuch that he made the carols for Christmas-eve and the religious plays for Corpus Christi, which the boys of the village represented; and everybody said they were most excellent. When the people of the village saw the two scholars so suddenly habited like shepherds, they were amazed, and could not get at the cause that induced them to make that strange alteration in their dress. About this time the father of Chrysostom died, and he inherited a large estate, in lands and goods, flocks, herds, and money, of all which the youth remained absolute master; and, indeed, he deserved it all, for he was a very good companion, a charitable man, and a friend to those that were good, and had a face like any blessing.

Afterwards it came to be known that he changed his habit for no other purpose but that he might wander about these desert places after that shepherdess Marcela, with whom, as our lad told you, he was in love.

"As all that I have related is certain truth, I can more readily believe what our companion told us concerning the cause of Chrysostom's death; and therefore I advise you, sir, not to fail being to-morrow at his funeral, which will be very well worth seeing; for Chrysostom had a great many friends, and it is not half a league hence to the place of interment appointed by himself."

"I will certainly be there," said Don Quixote, "and I thank you for the pleasure you have given me by the recital of so entertaining a story."

Morning scarcely had dawned through the balconies of the east, when five of the six goatherds got up and went to awake Don Quixote, whom they asked whether he continued in his resolution of going to see the famous interment of Chrysostom, for, if so, they would bear him company. Don Quixote, who desired nothing more, arose, and ordered Sancho to saddle and pannel immediately, which he did with great expedition; and with the same dispatch they all set out on their journey.

They had not gone a quarter of a league, when upon crossing a pathway, they saw six shepherds advancing towards them, clad in jackets of black sheepskin, with garlands of cypress and bitter rosemary on their heads; each of them having in his hand a thick holly club. There came also with them two gentlemen on horseback, well equipped for travelling, who were attended by three lackeys on foot. When the two parties met they courteously saluted each other, and finding upon inquiry that all were proceeding to the place of burial, they continued their journey together.

Proceeding on, they discerned through a cleft between two high mountains about twenty shepherds coming down, all clad in jerkins of black wool, and crowned with garlands, some of which were of yew, and some of cypress. Six of them carried a bier covered with various flowers and boughs. One of the goatherds said: "Those who come hither are bearing the corpse of Chrysostom, and at the foot of yonder mountain is the place where he desired to be interred." Four of them, with sharp pickaxes, were making the grave by the side of a sharp rock. Upon the bier lay a dead body, strewed with flowers, in the dress of a shepherd, apparently about thirty years of age; and though dead, it was evident that his countenance had been beautiful and his figure elegant. Several books and a great number of papers, some open and some folded, lay round him on the bier. All that were present, spectators as well as those who were opening the grave, kept a marvellous silence, until one said to another: "Observe carefully, Ambrosio, whether this be the place which Chrysostom mentioned since you wish to be so exact in executing his will."

"It is here," answered Ambrosio; "for in this very place my unhappy friend often told me of his woe. Here it was, he told me, that he first beheld that mortal enemy of the human race; here it was that he declared to her his no less honorable than ardent passion; here it was that Marcela finally undeceived and treated him with such disdain that she put an end to the tragedy of his miserable life; and here, in memory of so many misfortunes, he desired to be deposited in the bowels of eternal oblivion."

Then, addressing himself to Don Quixote and the travellers, he thus continued: "This body, sirs, which you are regarding with compassionate eyes, was the receptacle of a soul upon which Heaven had bestowed an infinite portion of its treasures; this is the body of Chrysostom, who was a man of rare genius, matchless courtesy, and unbounded kindness; he was a phœnix in friendship, magnificent without ostentation, grave without arrogance, cheerful without meanness; in short, the first in all that was good, and second to none in all that was unfortunate. He loved, and was abhorred; he adored, and was scorned; he courted a savage; he solicited a statue; he pursued the wind; he called aloud to the desert; he was the slave of ingratitude, whose recompense was to leave him, in the middle of his career of life, a prey to death, inflicted by a certain shepherdess, whom he endeavored to render immortal in the memories of men; as these papers you are looking at would sufficiently demonstrate, had he not ordered me to commit them to the flames at the same time that his body was deposited in the earth."

"You would then be more rigorous and cruel to them," said Vivaldo, "than their master himself.

"It is neither just nor wise to fulfil the will of him who commands what is utterly unreasonable.

"Augustus Cæsar deemed it wrong to consent to the execution of what the divine Mantuan commanded in his will; therefore, Signor Ambrosio, although you commit your friend's body to the earth, do not commit his writings also to oblivion; and if he has ordained like a man aggrieved, do not you fulfil like one without discretion, but rather preserve those papers, in order that the cruelty of Marcela may be still remembered, and serve for an example to those who shall live in times to come, that they may avoid falling down the like precipices; for I am acquainted, as well as my companions here, with the story of this your enamored and despairing friend; we know also your friendship, and the occasion of his death, and what he ordered on his deathbed; from which lamentable history we may conclude how great has been the cruelty of Marcela, the love of Chrysostom, and the sincerity of your friendship; and also learn the end of those who run headlong in the path that delirious passion presents to their view. Last night we heard of Chrysostom's death, and that he was to be interred in this place; led, therefore, by curiosity and compassion, we turned out of our way, and determined to behold with our eyes what had interested us so much in the recital; and, in return for our pity, and our desire to give aid, had it been possible, we beseech you, oh wise Ambrosio—at least I request it on my own behalf—that you will not burn the papers, but allow me to take some of them."

Then, without waiting for the shepherd's reply, he stretched out his hand and took some of those that were nearest to him: upon which Ambrosio said: "Out of civility, signor, I will consent to your keeping those you have taken; but if you expect that I shall forbear burning those that remain, you are deceived."

Vivaldo, desirous of seeing what the papers contained, immediately opened one of them, and found that it was entitled, "The Song of Despair." Ambrosio, hearing it, said: "This is the last thing which the unhappy man wrote; and that all present may conceive, signor, to what a state of misery he was reduced, read it aloud; for you will have time enough while they are digging the grave."

"That I will do with all my heart," said Vivaldo; and, as all the bystanders had the same desire, they assembled around him, and he read in an audible voice as follows:—

Chrysostom's song.

i.

Since, cruel maid, you force me to proclaim

From clime to clime, the triumph of your scorn,

Let hell itself inspire my tortured breast

With mournful numbers, and untune my voice;

Whilst the sad pieces of my broken heart

Mix with the doleful accents of my tongue,

At once to tell my griefs and thy exploits,

Hear, then, and listen with attentive ear—

Not to harmonious sounds, but echoing groans,

Fetched from the bottom of my laboring breast,

To ease, in spite of thee, my raging smart.

ii.

The lion's roar, the howl of midnight wolves,

The scaly serpent's hiss, the raven's croak,

The burst of fighting winds that vex the main,
The widowed owl and turtle's plaintive moan,
With all the din of hell's infernal crew,
From my grieved soul forth issue in one sound—
Leaving my senses all confused and lost.
For ah! no common language can express
The cruel pains that torture my sad heart.
iii.
Yet let not Echo bear the mournful sounds
To where old Tagus rolls his yellow sands,

Or Betis, crowned with olives, pours his flood,
But here, 'midst rocks and precipices deep,
Or to obscure and silent vales removed,
On shores by human footsteps never trod,
Where the gay sun ne'er lifts his radiant orb,
Or with the envenomed face of savage beasts
That range the howling wilderness for food,
Will I proclaim the story of my woes—
Poor privilege of grief!—while echoes hoarse
Catch the sad tale, and spread it round the world.
iv.
Disdain gives death; suspicions, true or false,
O'erturn the impatient mind: with surer stroke
Fell jealousy destroys; the pangs of absence
No lover can support; nor firmest hope
Can dissipate the dread of cold neglect;
Yet I, strange fate! though jealous, though disdained,
Absent, and sure of cold neglect, still live.
And amidst the various torments I endure,

No ray of hope e'er darted on my soul,
Nor would I hope; rather in deep despair
Will I sit down, and, brooding o'er my griefs,
Vow everlasting absence from her sight.
v.
Can hope and fear at once the soul possess,
Or hope subsist with surer cause of fear?
Shall I, to shut out frightful jealousy,
Close my sad eyes, when every pang I feel
Presents the hideous phantom to my view?

What wretch so credulous but must embrace
Distrust with open arms, when he beholds
Disdain avowed, suspicions realized,
And truth itself converted to a lie?
Oh, cruel tyrant of the realm of love,
Fierce Jealousy, arm with a sword this hand,
Or thou, Disdain, a twisted cord bestow!
vi.
Let me not blame my fate; but, dying, think
The man most blest who loves, the soul most free
That love has most enthralled. Still to my thoughts
Let fancy paint the tyrant of my heart
Beauteous in mind as face, and in myself
Still let me find the source of her disdain,
Content to suffer, since imperial Love
By lover's woes maintains his sovereign state.
With this persuasion, and the fatal noose,
I hasten to the doom her scorn demands,
And, dying, offer up my breathless corse,

Uncrowned with garlands, to the whistling winds.

vii.

Oh thou, whose unrelenting rigor's force
First drove me to despair, and now to death;
When the sad tale of my untimely fall
Shall reach thy ear, though it deserve a sigh,
Veil not the heaven of those bright eyes in grief,
Nor drop one pitying tear, to tell the world
At length my death has triumphed o'er thy scorn:

With laughter and each circumstance of joy
The festival of my disastrous end.
Ah! need I bid thee smile? too well I know
My death's thy utmost glory and thy pride.

viii.

Come, all ye phantoms of the dark abyss:
Bring, Tantalus, thy unextinguished thirst,
And Sisyphus, thy still returning stone;
Come, Tityus, with the vulture at thy heart;
And thou, Ixion, bring thy giddy wheel;
Nor let the toiling sisters stay behind.
Pour your united griefs into this breast,
And in low murmurs sing sad obsequies
(If a despairing wretch such rites may claim)
O'er my cold limbs, denied a winding sheet.
And let the triple porter of the shades,
The sister Furies, and chimeras dire,
With notes of woe the mournful chorus join.
Such funeral pomp alone befits the wretch
By beauty sent untimely to the grave.

ix.

And thou, my song, sad child of my despair,

Complain no more; but since thy wretched fate

Improves her happier lot who gave thee birth,

Be all thy sorrows buried in my tomb.

None of the shepherds departed until, the grave being made and the papers burnt, the body of Chrysostom was interred, not without many tears from the spectators. They closed the sepulchre with a large fragment of a rock until a tombstone was finished, which Ambrosio said it was his intention to provide, and to inscribe upon it the following epitaph:—

chrysostom's epitaph.

The body of a wretched swain,

Killed by a cruel maid's disdain,

In this cold bed neglected lies.

He lived, fond, hapless youth! to prove

Th' inhuman tyranny of love,

Exerted in Marcela's eyes.

Then they strewed abundance of flowers and boughs on the grave, and after expressions of condolence to his friend Ambrosio, they took their leave of him.

All beauty does not inspire love; some please the sight without captivating the affections. If all beauties were to enamour and captivate, the hearts of mankind would be in a continual state of perplexity and confusion—for beautiful objects being infinite, the sentiments they inspire should also be infinite.

True love cannot be divided, and must be voluntary and unconstrained.

The viper deserves no blame for its sting, although it be mortal—because it is the gift of Nature.

Beauty in a modest woman is like fire or a sharp sword at a distance; neither doth the one burn nor the other wound those that come not too near them.

Honor and virtue are ornaments of the soul, without which the body, though it be really beautiful, ought not to be thought so.

Let him who is deceived complain.

Let him to whom faith is broken despair.

She who loves none can make none jealous, and sincerity ought not to pass for disdain.

Much time is necessary to know people thoroughly.

We are sure of nothing in this life.

There is no remembrance which time does not obliterate, nor pain which death does not terminate.

Fortune always leaves some door open in misfortune.

Sometimes we look for one thing and find another.

Self-praise depreciates.

The cat to the rat—the rat to the rope—the rope to the gallows.

Out of the frying-pan into the fire.

One man is no more than another, only inasmuch as he does more than another.

The lance never blunted the pen, nor the pen the lance.

A mouth without teeth is like a mill without a stone.

The dead to the bier, and the living to good cheer.

One effect of fear is to disturb the senses, and make things not to appear what they really are.

ADVENTURE OF THE DEAD BODY

They saw, advancing towards them, on the same road, a great number of lights, resembling so many moving stars. Sancho stood aghast at the sight of them, nor was Don Quixote unmoved. The one checked his ass and the other his horse, and both stood looking before them with eager attention. They perceived that the lights were advancing towards them, and that as they approached nearer they appeared larger. Sancho trembled like quicksilver at the sight, and Don Quixote's hair bristled upon his head; but, somewhat recovering himself, he exclaimed: "Sancho, this must be a most perilous adventure, wherein it will be necessary for me to exert my whole might and valor."

"Woe is me!" answered Sancho; "should this prove to be an adventure of goblins, as to me it seems to be, where shall I find ribs to endure?"

"Whatsoever phantoms they may be," said Don Quixote, "I will not suffer them to touch a thread of thy garment: for if they sported with thee before, it was because I could not get over the wall; but we are now upon even ground, where I can brandish my sword at pleasure."

"But, if they should enchant and benumb you, as they did then," quoth Sancho, "what matters it whether we are in the open field or not?"

"Notwithstanding that," replied Don Quixote, "I beseech thee, Sancho, to be of good courage; for experience shall give thee sufficient proof of mine."

"I will, if it please God," answered Sancho; and, retiring a little on one side of the road, and again endeavoring to discover what those walking lights might be, they soon after perceived a great many persons clothed in white.

This dreadful spectacle completely annihilated the courage of Sancho, whose teeth began to chatter, as if seized with a quartan ague; and his trembling and chattering increased as more of it appeared in view; for now they discovered about twenty persons in white robes, all on horseback, with lighted torches in their hands; behind them came a litter covered with black, which was followed by six persons in deep mourning; the mules on which they were mounted being covered likewise with black down to their heels; for that they were mules, and not horses, was evident by the slowness of their pace. Those robed in white were muttering to themselves in a low and plaintive tone.

This strange vision, at such an hour, and in a place so uninhabited might well strike terror into Sancho's heart, and even into that of his master; and so it would have done had he been any other than Don Quixote. As for Sancho, his whole stock of courage was now exhausted. But it was otherwise with his master, whose lively imagination instantly suggested to him that this must be truly a chivalrous adventure. He conceived that the litter was a bier, whereon was carried some knight sorely wounded, or slain, whose revenge was reserved for him alone; he, therefore, without delay couched his spear, seated himself firm in his saddle, and with grace and spirit advanced into the middle of the road by which the procession must pass; and, when they were near, he raised his voice and said: "Ho, knights, whoever ye are, halt, and give me an account to whom ye belong; whence ye come, whither ye are going, and what it is ye carry upon that bier; for in all appearance either ye have done some injury to others, or others to you: and it is expedient and necessary that I be informed of it, either to chastise ye for the evil ye have done, or to revenge ye of wrongs sustained."

"We are in haste," answered one in the procession; "the inn is a great way off, and we cannot stay to give so long an account as you require." Then, spurring his mule, he passed forward.

Don Quixote, highly resenting this answer, laid hold of his bridle and said: "Stand, and with more civility give me the account I demand; otherwise I challenge ye all to battle."

The mule was timid, and started so much upon his touching the bridle, that, rising on her hind legs, she threw her rider over the crupper to the ground. A lacquey that came on foot, seeing the man in white fall, began to revile Don Quixote, whose choler being now raised, he couched his spear, and immediately attacking one of the mourners, laid him on the ground grievously wounded; then turning about to the rest, it was worth seeing with what agility he attacked and defeated them; and it seemed as if wings at that instant had sprung on Rozinante—so lightly and swiftly he moved! All the white-robed people, being timorous and unarmed, soon quitted the skirmish and ran over the plain with their lighted torches, looking like so many masqueraders on a carnival or festival night. The mourners were so wrapped up and muffled in their long robes that they could make no exertion; so that Don Quixote, with entire safety, assailed them all, and, sorely against their will, obliged them to quit the field; for they thought him no man, but the devil from hell broke loose upon them to seize the dead body they were conveying in the litter.

All this Sancho beheld with admiration at his master's intrepidity, and said to himself: "This master of mine is certainly as valiant and magnanimous as he pretends to be."

A burning torch lay upon the ground near the first whom the mule had overthrown, by the light of which Don Quixote espied him, and going up to him, placed the point of his spear to his throat, commanding him to surrender, on pain of death. To which the fallen man answered: "I am surrendered enough already, since I cannot stir, for one of my legs is broken. I beseech you, sir, if you are a Christian gentleman, do not kill me: you would commit a great sacrilege, for I am a licentiate and have taken the lesser orders."

"Who the devil, then," said Don Quixote, "brought you hither, being an ecclesiastic?"

"Who, sir?" replied the fallen man; "my evil fortune."

"A worse fate now threatens you," said Don Quixote, "unless you reply satisfactorily to all my first questions."

"Your worship shall soon be satisfied," answered the licentiate; "and therefore you must know, sir, that though I told you before I was a licentiate, I am in fact only a bachelor of arts, and my name is Alonzo Lopez. I am a native of Alcovendas, and came from the city of Baeza with eleven more ecclesiastics, the same who fled with the torches. We were attending the corpse in that litter to the city of Segovia. It is that of a gentleman who died in

Baeza, where he was deposited till now, that, as I said before, we are carrying his bones to their place of burial in Segovia, where he was born."

"And who killed him?" demanded Don Quixote.

"God," replied the bachelor, "by means of a pestilential fever."

"Then," said Don Quixote, "our Lord hath saved me the labor of revenging his death, in case he had been slain by any other hand. But, since he fell by the hand of Heaven, there is nothing expected from us but patience and a silent shrug; for just the same must I have done had it been His pleasure to pronounce the fatal sentence upon me. It is proper that your reverence should know that I am a knight of La Mancha, Don Quixote by name, and that it is my office and profession to go over the world righting wrongs and redressing grievances."

He that seeketh danger perisheth therein.

Fear hath many eyes.

Evil to him that evil seeks.

Everybody has not discretion to take things by the right handle.

He loves thee well who makes thee weep.

THE GRAND ADVENTURE AND RICH PRIZE OF MAMBRINO'S HELMET

About this time it began to rain a little, and Sancho proposed entering the fulling-mill; but Don Quixote had conceived such an abhorrence of them for the late jest, that he would by no means go in: turning, therefore, to the right hand, they struck into another road, like that they had travelled through the day before. Soon after, Don Quixote discovered a man on horseback, who had on his head something which glittered as if it had been of gold; and scarcely had he seen it when, turning to Sancho, he said, "I am of opinion, Sancho, there is no proverb but what is true, because they are all sentences drawn from experience itself, the mother of all the sciences; especially that which says, 'Where one door is shut another is opened.' I say this because, if fortune last night shut the door against what we sought, deceiving us with the fulling-mills, it now opens wide another, for a better and more certain adventure; in which, if I am deceived, the fault will be mine, without imputing it to my ignorance of fulling-mills, or to the darkness of night. This I say because, if I mistake not, there comes one towards us who carries on his head Mambrino's helmet, concerning which thou mayest remember I swore the oath."

"Take care, sir, what you say, and more what you do," said Sancho; "for I would not wish for other fulling-mills, to finish the milling and mashing our senses."

"The devil take thee!" replied Don Quixote: "what has a helmet to do with fulling-mills?"

"I know not," answered Sancho; "but in faith, if I might talk as much as I used to do, perhaps I could give such reasons that your worship would see you are mistaken in what you say."

"How can I be mistaken in what I say, scrupulous traitor?" said Don Quixote. "Tell me, seest thou not yon knight coming towards us on a dapple-gray steed, with a helmet of gold on his head?"

"What I see and perceive," answered Sancho, "is only a man on a gray ass like mine, with something on his head that glitters."

"Why, that is Mambrino's helmet," said Don Quixote; "retire, and leave me alone to deal with him, and thou shalt see how, in order to save time, I shall conclude this adventure without speaking a word, and the helmet I have so much desired remain my own."

"I shall take care to get out of the way," replied Sancho; "but Heaven grant, I say again, it may not prove another fulling-mill adventure."

"I have already told thee, Sancho, not to mention those fulling-mills, nor even think of them," said Don Quixote: "if thou dost—I say no more, but I vow to mill thy soul for thee!" Sancho held his peace, fearing lest his master should perform his vow, which had struck him all of a heap.

Now the truth of the matter, concerning the helmet, the steed, and the knight which Don Quixote saw, was this. There were two villages in that neighborhood, one of them so small that it had neither shop nor barber, but the other adjoining to it had both; therefore the barber of the larger served also the less, wherein one customer now wanted to be let blood and another to be shaved; to perform which, the barber was now on his way, carrying with him his brass basin; and it so happened that while upon the road it began to rain, and to save his hat, which was a new one, he clapped the basin on his head, which being lately scoured was seen glittering at the distance of half a league; and he rode on a gray ass, as Sancho had affirmed. Thus Don Quixote took the barber for a knight, his ass for a dapple-gray steed, and his basin for a golden helmet; for whatever he saw was quickly adapted to his knightly extravagances: and when the poor knight drew near, without staying to reason the case with him, he advanced at Rozinante's best speed, and couched his lance, intending to run him through and through; but, when close upon him, without checking the fury of his career, he cried out, "Defend thyself, caitiff!

or instantly surrender what is justly my due."

The barber, so unexpectedly seeing this phantom advancing upon him, had no other way to avoid the thrust of the lance than to slip down from the ass; and no sooner had he touched the ground than, leaping up nimbler than a roebuck, he scampered over the plain with such speed that the wind could not overtake him. The basin he left on the ground; with which Don Quixote was satisfied, observing that the pagan had acted discreetly, and in imitation of the beaver, which, when closely pursued by the hunters, tears off with his teeth that which it knows by instinct to be the object of pursuit. He ordered Sancho to take up the helmet; who, holding it in his hand, said, "Before Heaven, the basin is a special one, and is well worth a piece of eight, if it is worth a farthing."

He then gave it to his master, who immediately placed it upon his head, turning it round in search of the visor; but not finding it he said, "Doubtless the pagan for whom this famous helmet was originally forged must have had a prodigious head—the worst of it is that one half is wanting."

When Sancho heard the basin called a helmet, he could not forbear laughing; which, however, he instantly checked on recollecting his master's late choler.

"What dost thou laugh at, Sancho?" said Don Quixote.

"I am laughing," answered he, "to think what a huge head the pagan had who owned that helmet, which is for all the world just like a barber's basin."

"Knowest thou, Sancho, what I conceive to be the case? This famous piece, this enchanted helmet, by some strange accident must have fallen into the possession of one who, ignorant of its true value as a helmet and seeing it to be of the purest gold, hath inconsiderately melted down the one-half for lucre's sake, and of the other half made this, which, as thou sayest, doth indeed look like a barber's basin; but to me, who know what it really is, its transformation is of no importance, for I will have it so repaired in the first town where there is a smith, that it shall not be surpassed nor even equalled by that which the god of smiths himself made and forged for the god of battles. In the mean time I will wear it as I best can, for something is better than nothing; and it will be sufficient to defend me from stones."

Be brief in thy discourse, for what is prolix cannot be pleasing.

Never stand begging for that which you have the power to take.

There are two kinds of lineages in the world. Some there are who derive their pedigree from princes and monarchs, whom time has gradually reduced until they have ended in a point, like a pyramid; others have had a low origin, and have risen by degrees, until they have become great lords. So that the difference is, that some have been what they now are not, and others are now what they were not before.

A leap from a hedge is better than the prayer of a bishop.

A snatch from behind a bush is better than the prayer of good men.

Customs come not all together, neither were they all invented at once.

Who sings in grief procures relief.

Let every one turn himself round, and look at home, and he will find enough to do.

To be grateful for benefits received is the duty of honest men—one of the sins that most offendeth God is ingratitude.

Benefits conferred on base-minded people are like drops of water thrown into the sea.

Retreating is not running away, nor is staying wisdom when the danger overbalances the hope; and it is the part of wise men to secure themselves to-day for to-morrow, and not to venture all upon one throw.

The wicked are always ungrateful.

Necessity urges desperate measures.

sonnet.

Know'st thou, O love, the pangs that I sustain,

Or, cruel, dost thou view those pangs unmov'd?

Or has some hidden cause its influence proved,

By all this sad variety of pain?

Love is a god, then surely he must know,

And knowing, pity wretchedness like mine;

From other hands proceeds the fatal blow—

Is then the deed, unpitying Chloe, thine?

Ah, no! a form so exquisitely fair

A soul so merciless can ne'er enclose.

From Heaven's high will my fate resistless flows,

And I, submissive, must its vengeance bear.

Nought but a miracle my life can save,

And snatch its destined victim from the grave.

The devil is subtle, and lays stumbling-blocks in our way, over which we fall without knowing how.

In all misfortunes the greatest consolation is a sympathizing friend.

Riches are but of little avail against the ills inflicted by the hand of Heaven.

He that buys and denies, his own purse belies.

Till you hedge in the sky, the starlings will fly.

If a painter would be famous in his art, he must endeavor to copy after the originals of the most excellent masters; the same rule is also applicable to all the other arts and sciences which adorn the commonwealth; thus, whoever aspires to a reputation for prudence and patience, must imitate Ulysses, in whose person and toils Homer draws a lively picture of those qualities; so also Virgil, in the character of Æneas, delineates filial piety, courage, and martial skill, being representations of not what they really were, but of what they ought to be, in order to serve as models of virtue to succeeding generations.

The absent feel and fear every ill.

"I have heard say," quoth Sancho, "'from hell there is no retention.'"

"I know not," said Don Quixote, "what retention means."

"Retention," answered Sancho, "means that he who is once in hell never does, nor ever can, get out again. I must strip off all my armor, and remain as naked as I was born, if I should determine upon imitating Orlando, in my penance, instead of Amadis."

While they were thus discoursing, they arrived at the foot of a high mountain, which stood separated from several others that surrounded it, as if it had been hewn out from them. Near its base ran a gentle stream, that watered a verdant and luxuriant vale, adorned with many wide-spreading trees, plants, and wild flowers of various hues. This was the spot in which the knight of the sorrowful figure chose to perform his penance; and, while contemplating the scene, he thus broke forth in a loud voice:—

"This is the place, O ye heavens! which I select and appoint for bewailing the misfortune in which ye have involved me. This is the spot where my flowing tears shall increase the waters of this crystal stream, and my sighs, continual and deep, shall incessantly move the foliage of these lofty trees, in testimony and token of the pain my persecuted heart endures. O ye rural deities, whoever ye be, that inhabit these remote deserts, give ear to the complaints of an unhappy lover, whom long absence and some pangs of jealousy have driven to bewail himself among these rugged heights, and to complain of the cruelty of that ungrateful fair, the utmost extent and ultimate perfection of all human beauty! O ye wood-nymphs and dryads, who are accustomed to inhabit the dark recesses of the mountain groves (so may the nimble and lascivious satyrs, by whom ye are wooed in vain, never disturb your sweet repose), assist me to lament my hard fate, or at least be not weary of hearing my groans! O my Dulcinea del Toboso, light of my darkness, glory of my pain, the north-star of my travels, and overruling planet of my fortune (so may Heaven listen to all thy petitions), consider, I beseech thee, to what a condition thy absence hath reduced me, and reward me as my fidelity deserves! O ye solitary trees, who henceforth are to be the companions of my retirement, wave gently your branches, to indicate that my presence does not offend you! And, O thou my squire, agreeable companion in my prosperous and adverse fortunes, carefully imprint on thy memory what thou shalt see me here perform, that thou mayest recount and recite it to her who is the sole cause of all!"

"There is no reason why you should threaten me," quoth Sancho, "for I am not a man to rob or murder anybody. Let every man's fate kill him, or God who made him. My master is doing a certain penance much to his liking in the midst of yon mountains."

Don Quixote took out the pocket-book, and, stepping aside, began with much composure to write the letter; and having finished, he called Sancho and said he would read it to him that he might have it by heart, lest he might perchance lose it by the way, for everything was to be feared from his evil destiny. To which Sancho answered: "Write it, sir, two or three times in the book, and give it me, and I will take good care of it; but to suppose that I can carry it in my memory is a folly, for mine is so bad that I often forget my own name. Your worship, however, may read it to me. I shall be glad to hear it, for it must needs be very much to the purpose."

"Listen, then," said Don Quixote, "this is what I have written ":—

Don quixote's letter to dulcinea del toboso.

High and Sovereign Lady:—He who is stabbed by the point of absence, and pierced by the arrows of love, O sweetest Dulcinea del Toboso, greets thee with wishes for that health which he enjoys not himself. If thy beauty despise me, if thy worth favor me not, and if thy disdain still pursue me, although inured to suffering, I shall ill support an affliction which is not only severe but lasting. My good squire Sancho will tell thee, O ungrateful fair and most beloved foe, to what a state I am reduced on thy account. If it be thy pleasure to relieve me, I am thine; if not, do what seemeth good to thee,—for by my death I shall at once appease thy cruelty and my own passion.

Until death thine,

The Knight of the Sorrowful Figure.

One should not talk of halters in the house of the hanged.

LINES DISCOVERED ON THE BARK OF A TREE, ADDRESSED TO DULCINEA DEL TOBOSO

Ye lofty trees, with spreading arms,

The pride and shelter of the plain;

Ye humble shrubs and flowery charms,

Which here in springing glory reign!

If my complaints may pity move,

Hear the sad story of my love!

While with me here you pass your hours,

Should you grow faded with my cares,

I'll bribe you with refreshing showers;

You shall be watered with my tears.

Distant, though present in idea,

I mourn my absent Dulcinea

Del Toboso.

Love's truest slave, despairing, chose

This lonely wild, this desert plain,

This silent witness of the woes

Which he, though guiltless, must sustain.

Unknowing why these pains he bears,

He groans, he raves, and he despairs.

With lingering fires Love racks my soul:

In vain I grieve, in vain lament;
Like tortured fiends I weep, I howl,
And burn, yet never can repent.
Distant, though present in idea,
I mourn my absent Dulcinea
Del Toboso.
While I through Honor's thorny ways,
In search of distant glory rove,
Malignant fate my toil repays
With endless woes and hopeless love.
Thus I on barren rocks despair,
And curse my stars, yet bless my fair.
Love, armed with snakes, has left his dart,
And now does like a fury rave;
And scourge and sting on every part,
And into madness lash his slave.
Distant, though present in idea,
I mourn my absent Dulcinea
Del Toboso.
When the stars are adverse, what is human power?

Who is there in the world that can boast of having fathomed and thoroughly penetrated the intricate and ever-changing nature of a woman?

What causes all my grief and pain?
Cruel disdain.
What aggravates my misery?
Accursed jealousy.

How has my soul its patience lost?
By tedious absence crossed.
Alas! no balsam can be found

> To heal the grief of such a wound.
>
> When absence, jealousy, and scorn
>
> Have left me hopeless and forlorn.
>
> What in my breast this grief could move?
>
> Neglected love.
>
> What doth my fond desires withstand?
>
> Fate's cruel hand.
>
> And what confirms my misery?
>
> Heaven's fixed decree.
>
> Ah me! my boding fears portend,
>
> This strange disease my life will end:
>
> For die I must, when three such foes,
>
> Heaven, fate, and love, my bliss oppose.
>
> My peace of mind, what can restore?
>
> Death's welcome hour.
>
> What gains love's joys most readily?
>
> Fickle inconstancy.
>
> Its pains what medicine can assuage?
>
> Wild frenzy's rage.
>
> 'Tis therefore little wisdom, sure,
>
> For such a grief to seek a cure,
>
> That knows no better remedy
>
> Than frenzy, death, inconstancy.

The hour, the season, the solitude, the voice, and the skill of the singer, all conspired to impress the auditors with wonder and delight, and they remained for some time motionless, in expectation of hearing more; but, finding the silence continue, they resolved to see who it was who had sung so agreeably, and were again detained by the same voice regaling their ears with this sonnet: —

> Friendship, thou hast with nimble flight
>
> Exulting gained the empyreal height,

In heaven to dwell, while here below

Thy semblance reigns in mimic show;

From thence to earth, at thy behest,

Descends fair peace, celestial guest!

Beneath whose veil of shining hue

Deceit oft lurks, concealed from view.

Leave, friendship! leave thy heavenly seat,

Or strip thy livery off the cheat.

If still he wears thy borrowed smiles,

And still unwary truth beguiles,

Soon must this dark terrestrial ball

Into its first confusion fall.

What is sudden death to a protracted life of anguish?

"O heavens! have I then at last found a place which may afford a secret grave for this wretched body? Yes, if the silence of this rocky desert deceive me not, here I may die in peace. Ah, woe is me! Here at least I may freely pour forth my lamentations to Heaven, and shall be less wretched than among men, from whom I should in vain seek counsel, redress, or consolation."

One evil produces another, and misfortunes never come singly.

O memory, thou mortal enemy of my repose! wherefore now recall to me the incomparable beauty of that adored enemy of mine! Were it not better, thou cruel faculty! to represent to my imagination her conduct at that period—that moved by so flagrant an injury, I may strive if not to avenge it, at least to end this life of pain?

For no grievance can harass or drive the afflicted to such extremity, while life remains, as to make them shut their ears against that counsel which is given with the most humane and benevolent intention.

Music lulls the disordered thoughts, and elevates the dejected spirits.

All women, let them be never so homely, are pleased to hear themselves celebrated for beauty.

The eyes of love or of idleness are like those of a lynx.

One mischance invites another, and the end of one misfortunep is often the beginning of a worse.

Among friends we ought not to stand upon trifles.

No man can command the first emotions of his passions.

Every new fault deserves a new penance.

Where is the wonder one devil should be like another?

Gifts are good after Easter.

A sparrow in the hand is worth more than a bustard on the wing.

He that will not when he may, when he would he shall have nay.

Men may prove and use their friends, and not presume upon their friendship in things contrary to the decrees of Heaven.

A man dishonored is worse than dead.

"I have heard it preached," quoth Sancho, "that God is to be loved with this kind of love, for Himself alone, without our being moved to it by hope of reward or fear of punishment; though, for my part, I am inclined to love and serve Him for what He is able to do for me."

"The devil take thee for a bumpkin," said Don Quixote; "thou sayest ever and anon such apt things that one would almost think thee a scholar."

"And yet, by my faith," quoth Sancho, "I cannot so much as read."

Squires and knight-errants are subject to much hunger and ill-luck.

A man on whom Heaven has bestowed a beautiful wife should be as cautious respecting the friends he introduces at home as to her female acquaintance abroad.

If from equal parts we take equal parts, those that remain are equal.

To attempt voluntarily that which must be productive of evil rather than good, is madness and folly. Difficult works are undertaken for the sake of Heaven, or of the world, or both: the first are such as are performed by the saints while they endeavor to live the life of angels in their human frames; such as are performed for love of the world are encountered by those who navigate the boundless ocean, traverse different countries and various climates to acquire what are called the goods of fortune. Those who assail hazardous enterprises for the sake of both God and man are brave soldiers, who no sooner perceive in the enemy's wall a breach made by a single cannon-ball, than, regardless of danger and full of zeal in the defence of their faith, their country, and their king, they rush where death in a thousand shapes awaits them. These are difficulties commonly attempted, and, though perilous, are glorious and profitable.

tears of st. peter.

Shame, grief, remorse, in Peter's breast increase,

Soon as the blushing morn his crime betrays;

When most unseen, then most himself he sees,

And with due horror all his soul surveys.

For a great spirit needs no censuring eyes

To wound his soul, when conscious of a fault;

But, self-condemn'd, and e'en self-punished, lies,

And dreads no witness like upbraiding Thought.

Expect not, therefore, by concealment, to banish sorrow; for, even though you weep not openly, tears of blood will flow from your heart. So wept that simple doctor, who, according to the poet, would venture to make a trial of the cup which the more prudent Rinaldo wisely declined doing; and although this be a poetical fiction, there is a concealed moral in it worthy to be observed and followed.

There is no jewel in the world so valuable as a chaste and virtuous woman. The honor of women consists in the good opinion of the world; and since that of your wife is eminently good, why would you have it questioned? Woman, my friend, is an imperfect creature; and, instead of laying stumbling-blocks in her way, we should clear the path before her, that she may readily attain that virtue which is essential in her. Naturalists inform us that the ermine is a little creature with extremely white fur, and that when the hunters are in pursuit of it, they spread with mire all the passes leading to its haunts, to which they then drive it, knowing that it will submit to be taken rather than defile itself. The virtuous and modest woman is an ermine, and her character whiter than snow; and in order to preserve it, a very different method must be taken from that which is used with the ermine.

The reputation of a woman may also be compared to a mirror of crystal, shining and bright, but liable to be sullied by every breath that comes near it. The virtuous woman must be treated like a relic—adored but not handled; she should be guarded and prized, like a fine flower-garden, the beauty and fragrance of which the owner allows others to enjoy only at a distance, and through iron rails.

The devil, when he would entrap a cautious person, assumes an angel form till he carries his point, when the cloven foot appears.

He who builds on impossibilities should be denied the privilege of any other foundation.

Hope is ever born with love.

Castles should not be left without governors, nor armies without generals.

The passion of love is to be conquered by flight alone; it is vain to contend with a power which, though human, requires more than human strength to subdue.

sonnet.

In the dead silence of the peaceful night,

When others' cares are hushed in soft repose,

The sad account of my neglected woes

To conscious Heaven and Chloris I recite.

And when the sun, with his returning light,

Forth from the east his radiant journey goes,

With accents such as sorrow only knows,

My griefs to tell is all my poor delight.

And when bright Phœbus from his starry throne

Sends rays direct upon the parched soil,

Still in the mournful tale I persevere;

Returning night renews my sorrow's toil;

And though from morn to night I weep and moan,

Nor Heaven nor Chloris my complainings hear.

Are we to take all that enamored poets sing for truth?

sonnet.

Believe me, nymph, I feel th' impending blow,

And glory in the near approach of death;

For when thou see'st my corse devoid of breath,

My constancy and truth thou sure wilt know,

Welcome to me Oblivion's shade obscure!

Welcome the loss of fortune, life, and fame!

But thy loved features, and thy honored name,

Deep graven on my heart, shall still endure.

And these, as sacred relics, will I keep

Till that sad moment when to endless night

My long-tormented soul shall take her flight

Alas for him who on the darkened deep

Floats idly, sport of the tempestuous tide,

No port to shield him, and no star to guide!

He who gives freely gives twice.

That which is lightly gained is little valued.

For love sometimes flies and sometimes walks—runs with one person, and goes leisurely with another: some he warms, and some he burns; some he wounds, and others he kills: in one and the same instant he forms and accomplishes his projects. He often in the morning lays siege to a fortress which in the evening surrenders to him—for no force is able to resist him.

Heaven always favors the honest purpose.

Rank is not essential in a wife.

True nobility consists in virtue.

It is no derogation to rank to elevate beauty adorned with virtue.

Time will discover.

"Certainly, gentlemen, if we rightly consider it, those who make knight-errantry their profession often meet with surprising and most stupendous adventures. For what mortal in the world, at this time entering within this castle, and seeing us sit together as we do, will imagine and believe us to be the same persons which in reality we are? Who is there that can judge that this lady by my side is the great queen we all know her to be, and that I am that Knight of the Sorrowful Figure so universally made known by fame? It is, then, no longer to be doubted but that this exercise and profession surpasses all others that have been invented by man, and is so much the more honorable as it is more exposed to dangers. Let none presume to tell me that the pen is preferable to the sword. This may be ascertained by regarding the end and object each of them aims at; for that intention is to be most valued which makes the noblest end its object. The scope and end of learning, I mean human learning (in this place I speak not of divinity, whose aim is to guide souls to Heaven, for no other can equal a design so infinite as that), is to give a perfection to distribute justice, bestowing upon every one his due, and to procure and cause good laws to be observed; an end really generous, great, and worthy of high commendation, but yet not equal to that which knight-errantry tends to, whose object and end is peace, which is the greatest blessing man can wish for in this life. And, therefore, the first good news that the world received was that which the angels brought in the night—the beginning of our day—when they sang in the air, 'Glory to God on high, peace on earth, and to men good-will.' And the only manner of salutation taught by our great Master to His friends and favorites was, that entering any house they should say, 'Peace be to this house.' And at other times He said to them, 'My peace I give to you,' 'My peace I leave to you,' 'Peace be among you.' A jewel and legacy worthy of such a donor, a jewel so precious that without it there can be no happiness either in earth or heaven. This peace is the true end of war; for arms and war are one and the same thing. Allowing, then, this truth, that the end of war is peace, and that in this it excels the end of learning, let us now weigh the bodily labors the scholar undergoes against those the warrior suffers, and then see which are the greatest.

"These, then, I say, are the sufferings and hardships a scholar endures. First, poverty (not that they are all poor, but to urge the worst that may be in this case); and having said he endures poverty, methinks nothing more need be urged to express his misery; for he that is poor enjoys no happiness, but labors under this poverty in all its parts, at one time in hunger, at another in cold, another in nakedness, and sometimes in all of them together; yet his poverty is not so great, but still he eats, though it be later than the usual hour, and of the scraps of the rich; neither can the scholar miss of somebody's stove or fireside to sit by; where, though he be not thoroughly heated, yet he may gather warmth, and at last sleep away the night under a roof. I will not touch upon other less material circumstances, as the want of linen, and scarcity of shoes, thinness and baldness of their clothes, and their surfeiting when good fortune throws a feast in their way; this is the difficult and uncouth path they tread, often stumbling and falling, yet rising again and pushing on, till they attain the preferment they aim at; whither being arrived, we have seen many of them, who, having been carried by a fortunate gale through all these quick-sands, from a chair govern the world; their hunger being changed into satiety, their cold into comfortable warmth, their nakedness into magnificence of apparel, and the mats they used to lie upon, into stately beds of costly silks and softest linen, a reward due to their virtue. But yet their sufferings, being compared to those the soldier endures, appear much inferior, as I shall in the next place make out."

Don Quixote, after a short pause, continued his discourse thus:—"Since, in speaking of the scholar, we began with his poverty and its several branches, let us see whether the soldier be richer. We shall find that poverty itself is not more poor: for he depends on his wretched pay, which comes late, and sometimes never; or upon what he can pillage, at the imminent risk of his life and conscience. Such often is his nakedness that his slashed buff-doublet serves him both for finery and shirt; and in the midst of winter, on the open plain, he has nothing to warm him but the breath of his mouth, which, issuing from an empty place, must needs be cold. But let us wait, and see whether night will make amends for these inconveniences: if his bed be too narrow it is his own fault, for he may measure out as many feet of earth as he pleases, and roll himself thereon at pleasure without fear of rumpling the sheets. Suppose the moment arrived of taking his degree—I mean, suppose-the day of battle come: his doctoral cap may then be of lint, to cover some gun-shot wound, which perhaps has gone through his temples, or deprived him of an arm or leg.

"And even suppose that Heaven in its mercy should preserve him alive and unhurt, he will probably remain as poor as ever; for he must be engaged and victorious in many battles before he can expect high promotion; and such good fortune happens only by a miracle: for you will allow, gentlemen, that few are the number of those that have reaped the reward of their services, compared with those who have perished in war. The dead are countless; whereas those who survived to be rewarded may be numbered with three figures. Not so with scholars, who by their salaries (I will not say their perquisites) are generally handsomely provided for. Thus the labors of the soldier are greater, although his reward is less. It may be said in answer to this, that it is easier to reward two thousand scholars than thirty thousand soldiers: for scholars are rewarded by employments which must of course be given to men of their profession; whereas the soldier can only be rewarded by the property of the master whom, he serves; and this defence serves to strengthen my argument.

"But, waiving this point, let us consider the comparative claims to pre-eminence: for the partisans of each can bring powerful arguments in support of their own cause. It is said in favor of letters that without them arms could not subsist; for war must have its laws, and laws come within the province of the learned. But it may be alleged in reply, that arms are necessary to the maintenance of law; by arms the public roads are protected, cities guarded, states defended, kingdoms preserved, and the seas cleared of corsairs and pirates. In short, without arms there would be no safety for cities, commonwealths or kingdoms. Besides, it is just to estimate a pursuit in proportion to the cost of its attainment. Now it is true that eminence in learning is purchased by time, watching, hunger, nakedness, vertigo, indigestion, and many other inconveniences already mentioned; but a man who rises gradually to be a good soldier endures all these, and far more. What is the hunger and poverty which menace the man of letters compared with the situation of the soldier, who, besieged in some fortress, and placed as sentinel in some ravelin or cavalier, perceives that the enemy is mining toward the place where he stands, and yet he must on no account stir from his post or shun the imminent danger that threatens him? All that he can do in such a case is to give notice to his officer of what passes, that he may endeavor to counteract it; in the meantime he must stand his ground, in momentary expectation of being mounted to the clouds without wings, and then dashed headlong to the earth. And if this be thought but a trifling danger, let us see whether it be equalled or exceeded by the encounter of two galleys, prow to prow, in the midst of the white sea, locked and grappled together, so that there is no more room left for the soldier than the two-foot plank at the break-head; and though he sees as many threatening ministers of death before him as there are pieces of artillery pointed at him from the opposite side, not the length of a lance from his body; though he knows that the first slip of his foot sends him to the bottom of the sea; yet, with an undaunted heart, inspired by honor, he exposes himself as a mark to all their fire, and endeavors by that narrow pass to force his way into the enemy's vessel! And, what is most worthy of admiration, no sooner is one fallen, never, to rise again in this world, than another takes his place; and if he also fall into the sea, which lies in wait to devour him, another and another succeeds without intermission! In all the extremities of war there is no example of courage and intrepidity to exceed this. Happy those ages which knew not the dreadful fury of artillery!—those instruments of hell (where, I verily believe, the inventor is now receiving the reward of his diabolical ingenuity), by means of which the cowardly and the base can deprive the bravest soldier of life. While a gallant spirit animated with heroic ardor is pressing to glory, comes a chance ball, sent by one who perhaps fled in alarm at the flash of his own accursed weapon, and in an instant cuts short the life of him who deserved to live for ages! When I consider this, I could almost repent having undertaken this profession of knight-errantry in so detestable an age; for though no danger can daunt me, still it gives me some concern to think that powder and lead may suddenly cut short my career of glory. But Heaven's will be done! I have this satisfaction, that I shall acquire the greater fame if I succeed, inasmuch as the perils by which I am beset are greater than those to which the knights-errant of past ages were exposed."

The army is a school in which the miser becomes generous, and the generous prodigal.

A covetous soldier is a monster which is rarely seen.

Liberality may be carried too far in those who have children to inherit from them.

How seldom promises made in slavery are remembered after a release from bondage.

Good fortune seldom comes pure and single, unattended by some troublesome or unexpected circumstance.

Though we love the treason we abhor the traitor.

What transport in life can equal that which a man feels on the restoration of his liberty?

"The church, the court, or the sea;" as if it more fully expressed the following advice,—He that would make his fortune, ought either to dedicate his time to the church, go to sea as a merchant, or attach himself to the court: for it is commonly observed, that "the king's crumb is worth the baron's batch."

sonnet upon the goleta.

O happy souls, by death at length set free

From the dark prison of mortality,

By glorious deeds, whose memory never dies—

From earth's dim spot exalted to the skies!

What fury stood in every eye confessed!

What generous ardor fired each manly breast,

While slaughtered heaps distained the sandy shore,

And the tinged ocean blushed with hostile gore!

O'erpowered by numbers, gloriously ye fell:

Death only could such matchless courage quell;

Whilst dying thus ye triumphed o'er your foes—

Its fame the world, its glory heaven, bestows!

sonnet on the fort.

From 'midst these walls, whose ruins spread around,

And scattered clods that heap the ensanguined ground,

Three thousand souls of warriors, dead in fight,

To better regions took their happy flight.

Long with unconquered souls they bravely stood,

And fearless shed their unavailing blood:

Till, to superior force compelled to yield,

Their lives they quitted in the well-fought field.
This fatal soil has ever been the tomb
Of slaughtered heroes, buried in its womb:
Yet braver bodies did it ne'er sustain,
Nor send more glorious soul the skies to gain.

i.

Tossed in a sea of doubts and fears,
Love's hapless mariner, I sail,
Where no inviting port appears,
To screen me from the stormy gale.

ii.

At distance viewed, a cheering star
Conducts me through the swelling tide;
A brighter luminary, far,
Than Palinurus o'er descried.

iii.

My soul, attracted by its blaze,
Still follows where it points the way,
And while attentively I gaze,
Considers not how far I stray.

iv.

But female pride, reserved and shy,
Like clouds that deepen on the day,
Oft shroud it from my longing eye,
When most I need the genial ray.

v.

O lovely star, so pure and bright!
Whose splendor feeds my vital fire,
The moment thou deny'st thy light,

Thy lost adorer will expire!

song.

Unconquered hope, thou bane of fear,

And last deserter of the brave,

Thou soothing ease of mortal care,

Thou traveller beyond the grave;

Thou soul of patience, airy food,

Bold warrant of a distant good,

Reviving cordial, kind decoy;

Though fortune frowns and friends depart,

Though Silvia flies me, flattering joy,

Nor thou, nor love, shall leave my doting heart.

No slave, to lazy ease resigned,

E'er triumphed over noble foes;

The monarch fortune most is kind

To him who bravely dares oppose.

They say, Love rates his blessing high,

But who would prize an easy joy?

My scornful fair then I'll pursue,

Though the coy beauty still denies;

I grovel now on earth, 'tis true,

But, raised by her, the humble slave may rise.

Might overcomes.

Him to whom God giveth may St. Peter bless.

Diligence is the mother of success, and in many important causes experience hath shown that the assiduity of the solicitor hath brought a very doubtful suit to a very fortunate issue; but the truth of this maxim is nowhere more evinced than in war, where activity and despatch anticipate the designs of the enemy, and obtain the victory before he has time to put himself in a posture of defence.

The common adage that delays are dangerous acts as spurs upon the resolution.

There are more tricks in the town than are dreamt of.

Virtue is always more persecuted by the wicked than beloved by the righteous.

Virtue is so powerful that of herself she will, in spite of all the necromancy possessed by the first inventor, Zoroaster, come off conqueror in every severe trial, and shine refulgent in the world, as the sun shines in the heavens.

Fables should not be composed to outrage the understanding; but by making the wonderful appear possible, and creating in the mind a pleasing interest, they may both surprise and entertain; which cannot be effected where no regard is paid to probability. I have never yet found a regular, well-connected fable in any of our books of chivalry—they are all inconsistent and monstrous; the style is generally bad; and they abound with incredible exploits, lascivious amours, absurd sentiment, and miraculous adventures; in short, they should be banished every Christian country.

Just are virtue's fears where envy domineers.

Bounty will not stay where niggards bear the sway.

Fortune turns faster than a mill-wheel, and those who were yesterday at top, may find themselves at bottom to-day.

Every one is the son of his own works.

The mind receives pleasure from the beauty and consistency of what is presented to the imagination, not from that which is incongruous and unnatural.

Fiction is always the better the nearer it resembles truth, and agreeable in proportion to the probability it bears and the doubtful credit which it inspires. Wherefore, all such fables ought to be suited to the understanding of those who read them, and written so as that, by softening impossibilities, smoothing what is rough, and keeping the mind in suspense, they may surprise, agreeably perplex, and entertain, creating equal admiration and delight; and these never can be excited by authors who forsake probability and imitation, in which the perfection of writing consists.

Epics may be written in prose as well as verse.

To assert that there never was an Amadis in the world, nor any other of the knights-adventurers of whom so many records remain, is to say that the sun does not enlighten, the frost produce cold, nor the earth yield sustenance.

The approbation of the judicious few should far outweigh** the censure of the ignorant.

An author had better be applauded by the few that are wise, than laughed at by the many that are foolish.

Our modern plays, not only those which are formed upon fiction, but likewise such as are founded on the truth of history, are all, or the greatest part, universally known to be monstrous productions, without either head or tail, and yet received with pleasure by the multitude, who approve and esteem them as excellent performances, though they are far from deserving that title; and if the authors who compose, and the actors who represent them, affirm that this and no other method is to be practised, because the multitude must be pleased; that those which bear the marks of contrivance, and produce a fable digested according to the rules of art, serve only for entertainment to four or five people of taste, who discern the beauties of the plan, which utterly escape the rest of the audience; and that it is better for them to gain a comfortable livelihood by the many, than starve upon reputation with the few; at this rate, said I, if I should finish my book, after having scorched every hair in my whiskers in poring over it, to preserve those rules and precepts already mentioned, I might fare at last like the sagacious botcher, who sewed for nothing and found his customers in thread.

It is not a sufficient excuse to say that the object in permitting theatrical exhibitions being chiefly to provide innocent recreation for the people, it is unnecessary to limit and restrain the dramatic author within strict rules of composition; for I affirm that the same object is, beyond all comparison, more effectually attained by legitimate works. The spectator of a good drama is amused, admonished, and improved by what is diverting, affecting, and moral in the representation; he is cautioned against deceit, corrected by example, incensed against vice, stimulated to the love of virtue.

Comedy, according to Tully, ought to be the mirror of life, the exemplar of manners, and picture of truth; whereas those that are represented in this age are mirrors of absurdity, exemplars of folly, and pictures of lewdness; for sure, nothing can be more absurd in a dramatic performance, than to see the person, who, in the first scene of the first act, was produced a child in swaddling-clothes, appear a full-grown man with a beard in the second; or to represent an old man active and valiant, a young soldier cowardly, a footman eloquent, a page a counsellor, a king a porter, and a princess a scullion. Then what shall we say concerning their management of the time and place in which the actions have, or may be supposed to have happened? I have seen a comedy, the first act of which was laid in Europe, the second in Asia, and the third was finished in Africa; nay, had there been a fourth, the scene would have shifted to America, so that the fable would have travelled through all the four divisions of the globe. If imitation be the chief aim of comedy, how can any ordinary understanding be satisfied with seeing an action that passed in the time of King Pepin and Charlemagne, ascribed to the Emperor Heraclius, who, being the principal personage, is represented, like Godfrey of Boulogne, carrying the cross into Jerusalem, and making himself master of the holy sepulchre, an infinite number of years having passed between the one and the other? Or, when a comedy is founded upon fiction, to see scraps of real history introduced, and facts misrepresented both with regard to persons and times, not with any ingenuity of contrivance, but with the most manifest and inexcusable errors and stupidity; and what is worst of all, there is a set of ignorant pretenders who call this the perfection of writing, and that every attempt to succeed by a contrary method is no other than a wild-goose chase.

The bow cannot remain always bent; and relaxation, both of body and mind, is indispensable to all.

Can you deny what is in everybody's mouth, when a person is in the dumps? It is always then said, "I know not what such a one ails—he neither eats, nor drinks, nor sleeps, nor answers to the purpose, like other men—surely he is enchanted." Wherefore, it is clear that such, and such only, are enchanted who neither eat, nor drink, nor sleep, and not they who eat and drink when they can get it, and answer properly to all that is asked them.

The poor man is unable to exercise the virtue of liberality; and the gratitude which consists only in inclination is a dead thing, even as faith without works is dead. I shall, therefore, rejoice when fortune presents me with an opportunity of exalting myself, that I may show my heart in conferring benefits on my friends, especially on poor Sancho Panza here, my squire, who is one of the best men in the world; and I would fain bestow on him an earldom, as I have long since promised; although I am somewhat in doubt of his ability in the government of his estate.

Sancho, overhearing his master's last words, said: "Take you the trouble, Signor Don Quixote, to procure me that same earldom, which your worship has so often promised, and I have been so long waiting for, and you shall see that I shall not want ability to govern it. But even if I should, there are people, I have heard say, who farm these lordships; and paying the owners so much a year, take upon themselves the government of the whole, while his lordship lolls at his ease, enjoying his estate, without concerning himself any further about it. Just so will I do, and give myself no more trouble than needs mast, but enjoy myself like any duke, and let the world rub."

"This, brother Sancho," said the canon, "may be done, as far as regards the management of your revenue; but the administration of justice must be attended to by the lord himself, and requires capacity, judgment, and, above all, an upright intention, without which nothing prospers; for Heaven assists the good intent of the simple, and disappoints the evil designs of the cunning."

"I do not understand these philosophies," answered Sancho; "all that I know is, that I wish I may as surely have the earldom as I should know how to govern it; for I have as large a soul as another, and as large a body as the best of them; and I should be as much king of my own dominion as any other king; would do what I pleased; and, doing what I pleased, I should have my will; and having my will, I should be contented; and, being content, there is no more to be desired; and when there is no more to desire, there is an end of it."

"These are no bad philosophies, as you say, Sancho," quoth the canon; "nevertheless, there is a great deal more to be said upon the subject of earldoms."

"That may be," observed Don Quixote; "but I am guided by the numerous examples offered on this subject by knights of my own profession; who, in compensation for the loyal and signal services they had received from their squires, conferred upon them extraordinary favors, making them absolute lords of cities and islands: indeed, there was one whose services were so great that he had the presumption to accept of a kingdom. But why should I say more, when before me is the bright example of the great Amadis de Gaul, who made his squire knight of the Firm Island? Surely I may, therefore, without scruple of conscience, make an earl of Sancho Panza, who is one of the best squires that ever served knight-errant."

The mountains breed learned men, and the cottages of shepherds contain philosophers.

Upon the news of Don Quixote's arrival, Sancho Panza's wife repaired thither, and on meeting him, her first inquiry was whether the ass had come home well.

Sancho told her that he was in a better condition than his master.

"The Lord be praised," replied she, "for so great a mercy to me! But tell me, husband,** what good have you got by your squireship? Have you brought a petticoat home for me, and shoes for your children?"

"I have brought you nothing of that sort, dear wife," quoth Sancho; "but I have got other things of greater consequence."

"I am very glad of that," answered the wife, "pray show me your things of greater consequence, friend; for I would fain see them, to gladden my heart, which has been so sad, all the long time you have been away."

"You shall see them at home, wife," quoth Sancho, "and be satisfied at present; for if it please God that we make another sally in quest of adventures, you will soon see me an earl or governor of an island, and no common one either, but one of the best that is to be had."

"Grant Heaven it may be so, husband," quoth the wife, "for we have need enough of it. But pray tell me what you mean by islands; for I do not understand you."

"Honey is not for the mouth of an ass," answered Sancho: "in good time, wife, you shall see, yea, and admire to hear yourself styled ladyship by all your vassals."

"What do you mean, Sancho, by ladyship, islands, and vassals?" answered Teresa Panza; for that was Sancho's wife's name, though they were not of kin, but because it is the custom in La Mancha for the wife to take the husband's name.

"Be not in so much haste, Teresa, to know all this," said Sancho; "let it suffice that I tell you the truth, and sew up your mouth. But for the present know that there is nothing in the world so pleasant to an honest man, as to be squire to a knight-errant, and seeker of adventures. It is true indeed, most of them are not so much to a man's mind as he could wish; for ninety-nine of a hundred one meets with fall out cross and unlucky. This I know by experience; for I have sometimes come off tossed in a blanket, and sometimes well cudgelled. Yet, for all that, it is a fine thing to be in expectation of accidents, traversing mountains, searching woods, marching over rocks, visiting castles, lodging in inns, all at discretion, and the devil a farthing to pay."

Fame has preserved in the memoirs of La Mancha, that Don Quixote, the third time he sallied from home, went to Saragossa, where he was present at a famous tournament in that city, and that there befell him things worthy of his valor and good understanding. Nor would the chronicler have learned any thing concerning his death had he not fortunately become acquainted with an aged physician, who had in his custody a leaden box, found, as he said, under the ruins of an ancient hermitage then rebuilding: in which box was found a manuscript of parchment written in Gothic characters, but in Castilian verse, containing many of his exploits, and giving an account of the beauty of Dulcinea del Toboso, the figure of Rozinante, the fidelity of Sancho Panza, and the burial of Don Quixote himself, with several epitaphs and eulogies on his life and manners. All that could be read, and perfectly made out, were those inserted here by the faithful author of this strange and never-before-seen history; which author desires no other reward from those who shall read it, in recompense of the vast pains it has cost him to inquire into and search all the archives of La Mancha to bring it to light, but that they would afford him the same credit that ingenious people give to books of knight-errantry, which are so well received in the world; and herewith he will reckon himself well paid, and will rest satisfied; and will moreover be encouraged to seek and find out others, if not as true, at least of as much invention and entertainment. The first words, written in the parchment which was found in the leaden box, were these:—

The Academicians of Argamasilla,

A Town of la Mancha,

On the Life and Death of the Valorous

Don Quixote de la Mancha,

Hoc scripserunt.

Monicongo, Academician of Argamasilla, on the Sepulture of Don Quixote.

epitaph.

La Mancha's thunderbolt of war,

The sharpest wit and loftiest muse,

The arm which from Gaëta far

To Catai did its force diffuse;

He who, through love and valor's fire,

Outstripped great Amadis's fame

Bid warlike Galaor retire,

And silenced Belianis' name:

He who, with helmet, sword, and shield,

On Rozinante, steed well known,

Adventures fought in many a field,

Lies underneath this frozen stone.

Paniaguado, Academician of Argamasilla, in praise of Dulcinea Del Toboso.

sonnet.

She whom you see the plump and lusty dame,

With high erected chest and vigorous mien,

Was erst th' enamored knight Don Quixote's flame,

he fair Dulcinea, of Toboso, queen.

For her, armed cap-à-pie with sword and shield,

He trod the sable mountain o'er and o'er;

For her he traversed Montiel's well-known field,

And in her service toils unnumbered bore.

Hard fate! that death should crop so fine a flower!

And love o'er such a knight exert his tyrant power!

Caprichoso, a most ingenious Academician of Argamasilla, in praise of Don Quixote's Horse Rozinante.

sonnet.

On the aspiring adamantine trunk

Of a huge tree, whose root, with slaughter drunk

Sends forth a scent of war, La Mancha's knight,

Frantic with valor, and returned from fight,

His bloody standard trembling in the air,

Hangs up his glittering armor beaming far,

With that fine-tempered steel whose edge o'erthrows,

Hacks, hews, confounds, and routs opposing foes.

Unheard-of prowess! and unheard-of verse!

But art new strains invents, new glories to rehearse.

If Amadis to Grecia gives renown,

Much more her chief does fierce Bellona crown.

Prizing La Mancha more than Gaul or Greece,

As Quixote triumphs over Amadis.

Oblivion ne'er shall shroud his glorious name,

Whose very horse stands up to challenge fame!

Illustrious Rozinante, wondrous steed!

Not with more generous pride or mettled speed,

Or his mad lord, Orlando's Brilladore.

Burlador, the little Academician of Argamasilla, on Sancho Panza.

sonnet.

See Sancho Panza, view him well,
And let this verse his praises tell.
His body was but small, 'tis true,
Yet had a soul as large as two.
No guile he knew, like some before him
But simple as his mother bore him.
This gentle squire on gentle ass
Went gentle Rozinante's pace,
Following his lord from place to place.
To be an earl he did aspire,
And reason good for such desire;
But worth in these ungrateful times,
To envied honor seldom climbs.
Vain mortals! give your wishes o'er,
And trust the flatterer Hope no more,
Whose promises, whate'er they seem,
End in a shadow or a dream.

Cachidiablo, Academician of Argamasilla, on the Sepulture of Don Quixote.

epitaph.

Here lies an evil-errant knight,
Well bruised in many a fray,

Whose courser, Rozinante hight,
Long bore him many a way.
Close by his loving master's side
Lies booby Sancho Panza,
A trusty squire of courage tried,
And true as ever man saw.

Tiquitoc, Academician of Argamasilla, on the sepulture of Dulcinea del Toboso.

Dulcinea, fat and fleshy, lies

Beneath this frozen stone;

But, since to frightful death a prize,

Reduced to skin and bone.

Of goodly parentage she came,

And had the lady in her;

She was the great Don Quixote's flame,

But only death could win her.

These were all the verses that could be read: the rest, the characters being worm-eaten, were consigned to one of the Academicians, to find out their meaning by conjectures. We are informed he has done it, after many lucubrations and much pains, and that he designs to publish them, giving us hopes of Don Quixote's third sally.

"Forsi altro cantara con miglior plectro."

The noble mind may be clouded by adversity, but cannot be wholly concealed; for true merit shines by a light of its own, and, glimmering through the rents and crannies of indigence, is perceived, respected, and honored by the generous and the great.

A SHORT STORY OF WHAT HAPPENED ONCE IN SEVILLE.

A certain man, being deranged in his intellects, was placed by his relations in the mad-house of Seville. He had taken his degrees in the canon law at Ossuna; but had it been at Salamanca, many are of opinion he would, nevertheless, have been mad. This graduate, after some years' confinement, took into his head that he was quite in his right senses, and therefore wrote to the archbishop, beseeching him, with great earnestness and apparently with much reason, that he would be pleased to deliver him from that miserable state of confinement in which he lived; since, through the mercy of God, he had regained his senses; adding that his relations, in order to enjoy part of his estate, kept him still there, and, in spite of the clearest evidence, would insist upon his being mad as long as he lived.

The archbishop, prevailed upon by the many sensible epistles he received from him, sent one of his chaplains to the keeper of the mad-house to inquire into the truth of what the licentiate had alleged, and also to talk with him, and if it appeared that he was in his senses, to set him at liberty. The chaplain accordingly went to the rector, who assured him that the man was still insane, for though he sometimes talked very sensibly, it was seldom for any length of time without betraying his derangement; as he would certainly find on conversing with him. The chaplain determined to make the trial, and during the conversation of more than an hour, could perceive no symptom of incoherence in his discourse; on the contrary, he spoke with so much sedateness and judgment that the chaplain could not entertain a doubt of the sanity of his intellects. Among other things he assured him that the keeper was bribed by his relations to persist in reporting him to be deranged; so that his large estate was his great misfortune, to enjoy which his enemies had recourse to fraud, and pretended to doubt of the mercy of Heaven in restoring him from the condition of a brute to that of a man. In short, he talked so plausibly that he made the rector appear venal and corrupt, his relations unnatural, and himself so discreet that the chaplain determined to take him immediately to the archbishop, that he might be satisfied he had done right.

With this resolution the good chaplain desired the keeper of the house to restore to him the clothes which he wore when he was first put under his care. The keeper again desired him to beware what he did, since he might be assured that the licentiate was still insane; but the chaplain was not to be moved either by his cautions or entreaties; and as he acted by order of the archbishop, the keeper was compelled to obey him. The licentiate put on his new clothes, and now, finding himself rid of his lunatic attire, and habited like a rational creature, he entreated the chaplain, for charity's sake, to permit him to take leave of his late companions in affliction. Being desirous of seeing the lunatics who were confined in that house, the chaplain, with several other persons, followed him upstairs, and heard him accost a man who lay stretched in his cell outrageously mad; though just then composed and quiet. "Brother," said he to him, "have you any commands for me? for I am going to return to my own house, God having been pleased, of His infinite goodness and mercy, without any desert of mine, to restore me to my senses. I am now sound and well, for with God nothing is impossible; put your whole trust and confidence in Him, and he will doubtless restore you also. I will take care to send you some choice food; and fail not to eat it: for I have reason to believe, from my own experience, that all our distraction proceeds from empty stomachs, and brains filled with wind. Take heart, then, my friend, take heart; for despondence under misfortune impairs our health, and hastens our death."

This discourse was overheard by another madman, who was in an opposite cell; and raising himself up from an old mat, whereon he had thrown himself stark naked, he demanded aloud, who it was that was going away recovered and in his senses.

"It is I, brother," answered the licentiate, "that am going; for I need stay no longer here, and am infinitely thankful to heaven for having bestowed so great a blessing upon me."

"Take heed, licentiate, what you say, let not the devil delude you," replied the madman; "stir not a foot, but keep where you are, and you will spare yourself the trouble of being brought back."

"I know," replied the licentiate, "that I am perfectly well, and shall have no more occasion to visit the station churches."

"You well?" said the madman; "we shall soon see that; farewell! but I swear by Jupiter, whose majesty I represent on earth, that for this offence alone, which Seville is now committing, in carrying you out of this house, and judging you to be in your senses, I am determined to inflict such a signal punishment on this city, that the memory thereof shall endure for ever and ever, Amen. Know you not, little crazed licentiate, that I can do it, since, as I say, I am thundering Jupiter, who hold in my hands the flaming bolts, with which I can, and use, to threaten and destroy the world? But in one thing only will I chastise this ignorant people; and that is, there shall no rain fall on this town, or in all its district, for three whole years, reckoning from the day and hour in which this threatening is denounced. You at liberty, you recovered, and in your right senses! and I a madman, I distempered and in bonds! I will no more rain than I will hang myself."

All the bystanders were very attentive to the madman's discourse: but our licentiate, turning himself to our chaplain, and holding him by both hands, said to him: "Be in no pain, good sir, nor make any account of what this madman has said; for, if he is Jupiter and will not rain, I, who am Neptune, the father and the god of the waters, will rain as often as I please, and whenever there shall be occasion." To which the chaplain answered: "However, signor Neptune, it will not be convenient at present to provoke signor Jupiter; therefore, pray stay where you are; for, some other time, when we have a better opportunity and more leisure, we will come for you." The rector and the bystanders laughed; which put the chaplain half out of countenance. They disrobed the licentiate, who remained where he was; and there is an end of the story.

True valor lies in the middle, between the extremes of cowardice and rashness.

No padlocks, bolts, or bars can secure a maiden so well as her own reserve.

Honey is not for the mouth of an ass.

He must be blind, indeed, who cannot see through a sieve.

Comparisons, whether as to sense, courage, beauty, or rank, are always offensive.

Scruples of conscience afford no peace.

You have reckoned without your host.

When the head aches, all the members ache also.

Me pondra en la espina de Santa Lucia;—i. e., Will put me on St. Lucia's thorn; applicable to any uneasy situation.

Let every man lay his hand upon his heart, and not take white for black, nor black for white; for we are all as God made us, and oftentimes a great deal worse.

"First and foremost, then," said Sancho, "the common people take your worship for a downright madman, and me for no less a fool. The gentry say that, not content to keep to your own proper rank of a gentleman, you call yourself Don, and set up for a knight, with no more than a paltry vineyard and a couple of acres of land. The cavaliers say they do not choose to be vied with by those country squires who clout their shoes, and take up the fallen stitches of their black stockings with green silk."

"That," said Don Quixote, "is no reflection upon me; for I always go well clad, and my apparel is never patched; a little torn it may be, but more by the fretting of my armor than by time."

"As to your valor, courtesy, achievements, and undertakings," continued Sancho, "there are many different opinions. Some say you are mad, but humorous; others, valiant, but unfortunate; others, courteous, but absurd; and thus they pull us to pieces, till they leave neither your worship nor me a single feather upon our backs."

"Take notice, Sancho," said Don Quixote, "that, when virtue exists in an eminent degree, it is always persecuted."

"There cannot be a more legitimate source of gratification to a virtuous and distinguished man," said Don Quixote, "than to have his good name celebrated during his lifetime, and circulated over different nations; I say his good name, for if it were otherwise than good, death in any shape would be preferable."

To be represented otherwise than with approbation is worse than the worst of deaths.

There are as many different opinions as there are different tastes.

Pedir cotufas en el golfo, signifies to look for truffles in the sea, a proverb applicable to those who are too sanguine in their expectations and unreasonable in their desires.

"There is no necessity for recording actions which are prejudicial to the hero, without being essential to the history. It is not to be supposed that Æneas was in all his actions so pure as Virgil represents him, nor Ulysses so uniformly prudent as he is described by Homer."

"True," replied Sampson; "but it is one thing to write as a poet, and another to write as an historian. The poet may say or sing, not as things were, but as they ought to have been; but the historian must pen them not as they ought to have been, but as they really were, without adding to or diminishing aught from the truth."

There is no human history that, does not contain reverses of fortune.

Let every man take care how he speaks or writes of honest people, and not set down at a venture the first thing that comes uppermost.

"Sancho, thou art an arch rogue," replied Don Quixote, "and in faith, upon some occasions, hast no want of memory."

"Though I wanted ever so much to forget what my poor body has suffered," quoth Sancho, "the tokens that are still fresh on my ribs would not let me."

"Peace, Sancho," said Don Quixote, "and let signor bachelor proceed, that I may know what is further said of me in the history."

"And of me too," quoth Sancho, "for I hear that I am one of the principal parsons in it."

"Persons, not parsons, friend Sancho," quoth Sampson.

"What, have we another corrector of words?" quoth Sancho; "if we are to go on at this rate, we shall make slow work of it."

"As sure as I live, Sancho," answered the bachelor, "you are the second person of the history; nay, there are those who had rather hear you talk than the finest fellow of them all; though there are also some who charge you with being too credulous in expecting the government of that island promised you by Signor Don Quixote, here present."

"There is still sunshine on the wall," quoth Don Quixote; "and when Sancho is more advanced in age, with the experience that years bestow, he will be better qualified to be a governor than he is at present."

"'Fore Gad! sir," quoth Sancho, "if I am not fit to govern an island at these years, I shall be no better, able at the age of Methusalem. The mischief of it is, that the said island sticks somewhere else, and not in my want of a headpiece to govern it."

"Recommend the matter to God, Sancho," said Don Quixote, "and all will be well—perhaps better than thou mayst think; for not a leaf stirs on the tree without his permission."

"That is very true," quoth Sampson; "and if it please God, Sancho will not want a thousand islands to govern, much less one."

"I have seen governors ere now," quoth Sancho, "who, in my opinion, do not come up to the sole of my shoe; and yet they are called 'your lordship,' and eat their victuals upon plate."

With hay or with straw it is all the same.

Much knowledge and a mature understanding are requisite for an historian.

Wit and humor belong to genius alone.

The wittiest person in the comedy is he that plays the fool.

History is a sacred subject, because the soul of it is truth; and where truth is, there the divinity will reside; yet there are some who compose and cast off books as if they were tossing up a dish of pancakes.

There is no book so bad but something good may be found in it.

Printed works may be read leisurely, their defects easily seen, so they are scrutinized more or less strictly in proportion to the celebrity of the author.

"Men of great talents, whether poets or historians, seldom escape the attacks of those who, without ever favoring the world with any production of their own, take delight in criticising the works of others."

"Nor can we wonder at that," said Don Quixote, "when we observe the same practice among divines, who, though dull enough in the pulpit themselves, are wonderfully sharp-sighted in discovering the defects of other preachers."

"True, indeed, Signor Don Quixote," said Carrasco; "I wish critics would be less fastidious, nor dwell so much upon the motes which may be discerned even in the brightest works; for, though aliquando bonus dormitat Homerus, they ought to consider how much he was awake to produce a work with so much light and so little shade; nay, perhaps even his seeming blemishes are like moles, which are sometimes thought to be rather an improvement to beauty. But it cannot be denied that whoever publishes a book to the world, exposes himself to imminent peril, since, of all things, nothing is more impossible than to satisfy everybody. Above all, I would let my master know that, if he takes me with him, it must be upon condition that he shall battle it all himself, and that I shall only have to tend his person—I mean, look after his clothes and food; all which I will do with a hearty good-will; but if he expects I will lay hand to my sword, though it be only against beggarly woodcutters with hooks and hatchets, he is very much mistaken. I, Signor Sampson, do not set up for being the most valiant, but the best and most faithful squire that ever served knight-errant; and if my lord Don Quixote, in consideration of my many and good services, shall please to bestow on me some one of the many islands his worship says he shall light upon, I shall be much beholden to him for the favor; and if he give me none, here I am, and it is better to trust God than each other; and mayhap my government bread might not go down so sweet as that which I should eat without it; and how? do I know but the devil, in one of these governments, might set up a stumbling-block in my way, over which I might fall, and dash out my grinders? Sancho I was born, and Sancho I expect to die; yet for all that, if, fairly and squarely, without much care or much risk, Heaven should chance to throw an island, or some such thing, in my way, I am not such a fool neither as to refuse it; for, as the saying is, 'when the heifer is offered, be ready with the rope.'"

When good fortune knocks, make haste to bid her welcome.

"Brother Sancho," quoth the bachelor, "you have spoken like any professor; nevertheless, trust in Heaven and Signor Don Quixote, and then you may get not only an island but even a kingdom."

"One as likely as the other," answered Sancho, "though I could tell Signor Carrasco that my master will not throw the kingdom he gives me into a rotten sack; for I have felt my pulse, and find myself strong enough to rule kingdoms and govern islands; and so much I have signified before now to my master."

"Take heed, Sancho," quoth the bachelor, "for honors change manners; and it may come to pass, when you are a governor, that you may not know even your own mother."

"That," answered Sancho, "may be the case with those that are born among the mallows, but not with one whose soul, like mine, is covered four inches thick with the grace of an old Christian. No, no, I am not one of the ungrateful sort."

"Heaven grant it," said Don Quixote; "but we shall see when the government comes, and methinks I have it already in my eye."

Sancho went home in such high spirits that his wife observed his gayety a bow-shot off, insomuch that she could not help saying, "What makes you look so blithe, friend Sancho?"

To which he answered: "Would to Heaven, dear wife, I were not so well pleased as I seem to be!"

"I know not what you mean, husband," replied she, "by saying you wish you were not so much pleased; now, silly as I am, I cannot guess how any one can desire not to be pleased."

"Look you, Teresa," answered Sancho, "I am thus merry because I am about to return to the service of my master, Don Quixote, who is going again in search after adventures, and I am to accompany him, for so my fate wills it. Besides, I am merry with the hopes of finding another hundred crowns like those we have spent, though it grieves me to part from you and my children; and if Heaven would be pleased to give me bread, dryshod and at home, without dragging me over crags and cross-paths, it is plain that my joy would be better grounded, since it is now mingled with sorrow for leaving you; so that I was right in saying that I should be glad if it pleased Heaven I were not so Well pleased."

"Look you, Sancho," replied Teresa, "ever since you have been a knight-errant man you talk in such a roundabout manner that nobody can understand you."

"It is enough, wife," said Sancho, "that God understands me, for He is the understander of all things; and so much for that. And do you hear, wife, it behooves you to take special care of Dapple for these three or four days to come, that he may be in a condition to bear arms; so double his allowance, and get the pack-saddle in order and the rest of his tackling, for we are not going to a wedding, but to roam about the world and to give and take with giants, fiery dragons, and goblins, and to hear hissings, roarings, bellowings, and bleatings, all which would be but flowers of lavender if we had not to do with Yangueses and enchanted Moors."

"I believe, indeed, husband," replied Teresa, "that your squires-errant do not eat their bread for nothing, and therefore I shall not fail to beseech Heaven to deliver you speedily from so much evil hap."

"I tell you, wife," answered Sancho, "that did I not expect, ere long, to see myself governor of an island, I vow I should drop down dead upon the spot."

"Not so, good husband," quoth Teresa, "let the hen live, though it be with the pip. Do you live, and the devil take all the governments in the world! Without a government you came into the world, without a government you have lived till now, and without it you can be carried to your grave whenever it shall please God. How many folks are there in the world that have no government! and yet they live and are reckoned among the people. The best sauce in the world is hunger, and as that is never wanting to the poor, they always eat with a relish. But if, perchance, Sancho, you should get a government, do not forget me and your children. Consider that your son Sancho is just fifteen years old, and it is fit he should go to school if his uncle the abbot means to breed him up to the church. Consider, also, that Mary Sancha, your daughter, will not break her heart if we marry her; for I am mistaken if she has not as much mind to a husband as you have to a government. And verily say I, better a daughter but humbly married than highly kept."

"In good faith, dear wife," said Sancho, "if Heaven be so good to me that I get anything like a government, I will match Mary Sancha so highly that there will be no coming near her without calling her your ladyship."

"Not so, Sancho," answered Teresa, "the best way is to marry her to her equal; for if you lift her from clouted shoes to high heels, and instead of her russet coat of fourteenpenny stuff, give her a farthingale and petticoats of silk, and instead of plain Molly and thou she be called madam and your ladyship, the girl will not know where she is and will fall into a thousand mistakes at every step, showing her homespun country stuff."

"Peace, fool!" quoth Sancho, "she has only to practise two or three years and the gravity will set upon her as if it were made for her; and if not, what matters it? Let her be a lady, and come of it what will."

"Measure yourself by your condition, Sancho," answered Teresa, "and do not seek to raise yourself higher, but remember the proverb, 'Wipe your neighbor's son's nose and take him into your house.' It would be a pretty business, truly, to marry our Mary to some great count or knight, who, when the fancy takes him, would look upon her as some strange thing, and be calling her country-wench, clod-breaker's brat, and I know not what else. No, not while I live, husband; I have not brought up my child to be so used. Do you provide money, Sancho, and leave the matching of her to my care; for there is Lope Tocho, John Tocho's son, a lusty, hale young man, whom we know, and I am sure he has a sneaking kindness for the girl. To him she will be very well married, considering he is our equal, and will be always under our eye; and we shall be all as one, parents and children, grandsons and sons-in-law, and so the peace and blessing of Heaven will be among us all; and do not you be for marrying her at your courts and great palaces, where they will neither understand her nor she understand herself."

"Hark you, beast, and wife for Barabbas," replied Sancho, "why would you now, without rhyme or reason, hinder me from marrying my daughter with one who may bring me grandchildren that may be styled your lordships? Look you, Teresa, I have always heard my betters say, 'He that will not when he may, when he will he shall have nay'; and it would be wrong, now that fortune is knocking at our door, not to open it and bid her welcome. Let us spread our sail to the favorable gale, now that it blows.' ... Can't you perceive, animal, with half an eye," proceeded Sancho, "that I shall act wisely, in devoting this body of mine to some beneficial government that will lift us out of the dirt, and enable me to match Mary Sancha according to my own good pleasure; then wilt thou hear thyself called Donna Teresa Panza, and find thyself seated at church upon carpets, cushions, and tapestry, in despite and defiance of all the small gentry in the parish; and not be always in the same moping circumstances, without increase or diminution, like a picture in the hangings. But no more of this; Sanchica shall be a countess, though thou shouldst cry thy heart out."

"Look before you leap, husband," answered Teresa; "after all, I wish to God this quality of my daughter may not be the cause of her perdition; take your own way, and make her duchess or princess, or what you please; but I'll assure you it shall never be with my consent or good-will; I was always a lover of equality, my dear, and can't bear to see people hold their heads high without reason. Teresa was I christened, a bare and simple name, without the addition, garniture, and embroidery of Don or Donna; my father's name is Cascajo, and mine, as being your spouse, Teresa Panza, though by rights I should be called Teresa Cascajo; but as the king minds, the law binds; and with that name am I contented, though it be not burdened with a Don, which weighs so heavy that I should not be able to bear it. Neither will I put it in the power of those who see me dressed like a countess or governor's lady, to say: 'Mind Mrs. Porkfeeder, how proud she looks! it was but yesterday she toiled hard at the distaff, and went to mass with the tail of her gown about her head, instead of a veil; but now, forsooth, she has got her fine farthingales and jewels, and holds up her head as if we did not know her.' If God preserves me in my seven or five senses, or as many as they be, I shall never bring myself into such a quandary. As for your part, spouse, you may go to your governments and islands, and be as proud as a peacock; but as for my daughter and me, by the life of my father! we will not stir one step from the village; for, the wife that deserves a good name, stays at home as if she were lame; and the maid must be still a-doing, that hopes to see the men come awooing."

He that covers, discovers.

The poor man is scarcely looked at, while every eye is turned upon the rich; and if the poor man grows rich and great, then I warrant you there is work enough for your grumblers and backbiters, who swarm everywhere like bees.

"The first time, he was brought home to us laid athwart an ass, all battered and bruised. The second time he returned in an ox-wagon, locked up in a cage, and so changed, poor soul, that his own mother would not have known him; so feeble, wan, and withered, and his eyes sunk into the farthest corner of his brains, insomuch that it took me above six hundred eggs to get him a little up again, as Heaven and the world is my witness, and my hens, that will not let me lie."

"I can easily believe that," answered the bachelor; "for your hens are too well bred and fed to say one thing and mean another."

All objects present to the view exist, and are impressed upon the imagination with much greater energy and force, than those which we only remember to have seen.

When we see any person finely dressed, and set off with rich apparel and with a train of servants, we are moved to show him respect; for, though we cannot but remember certain scurvy matters either of poverty or parentage, that formerly belonged to him, but which being long gone by are almost forgotten, we only think of what we see before our eyes. And if, as the preacher said, the person so raised by good luck, from nothing, as it were, to the tip-top of prosperity, be well behaved, generous, and civil, and gives himself no ridiculous airs, pretending to vie with the old nobility, take my word for it, Teresa, nobody will twit him with what he was, but will respect him for what he is; except, indeed the envious, who hate every man's good luck.

People are always ready enough to lend their money to governors.

Clothe the boy so that he may look not like what he is, but what he may be.

To this burden women are born, they must obey their husbands if they are ever such blockheads.

He that's coy when fortune's kind, may after seek but never find.

All knights cannot be courtiers, neither can all courtiers be knights.

The courtier knight travels only on a map, without fatigue or expense; he neither suffers heat nor cold, hunger nor thirst; while the true knight-errant explores every quarter of the habitable world, and is by night and day, on foot or on horseback, exposed to all the vicissitudes of the weather.

All are not affable and well-bred; on the contrary, some there are extremely brutal and impolite. All those who call themselves knights, are not entitled to that distinction; some being of pure gold, and others of baser metal, notwithstanding the denomination they assume. But these last cannot stand the touch-stone of truth; there are mean plebeians, who sweat and struggle to maintain the appearance of gentlemen; and, on the other hand, there are gentlemen of rank who seem industrious to appear mean and degenerate; the one sort raise themselves either by ambition or virtue, while the other abase themselves by viciousness or sloth; so that we must avail ourselves of our understanding and discernment in distinguishing those persons, who, though they bear the same appellation, are yet so different in point of character. All the genealogies in the world may be reduced to four kinds. The first are those families who from a low beginning have raised and extended themselves, until they have reached the highest pinnacle of human greatness; the second are those of high extraction, who have preserved their original dignity; the third sort are those who, from a great foundation, have gradually dwindled, until, like a pyramid, they terminate in a small point. The last, which are the most numerous class, are those who have begun and continue low, and who must end the same.

Genealogies are involved in endless confusion, and those only are illustrious and great who are distinguished by their virtue and liberality, as well as their riches; for the great man who is vicious is only a great sinner, and the rich man who wants liberality is but a miserly pauper.

The gratification which wealth can bestow is not in mere possession, nor in lavishing it with prodigality, but in the wise application of it.

The poor knight can only manifest his rank by his virtues and general conduct. He must be well-bred, courteous, kind, and obliging; not proud nor arrogant; no murmurer. Above all, he must be charitable, and by two maravedis given cheerfully to the poor he shall display as much generosity as the rich man who bestows large alms by sound of bell. Of such a man no one would doubt his honorable descent, and general applause wall be the sure reward of his virtue.

There are two roads by which men may attain riches and honor: the one by letters, the other by arms.

The path of virtue is narrow, that of vice is spacious and broad; as the great Castilian poet expresses it:—

"By these rough paths of toil and pain

The immortal seats of bliss we gain,

Denied to those who heedless stray

In tempting pleasure's flowery way."

Fast bind, fast find.

He who shuffles is not he who cuts.

A bird in the hand is worth two in the bush.

Though there is little in a woman's advice, yet he that won't take it is not over-wise.

We are all mortal: here to-day and gone to-morrow.

The lamb goes to the spit as soon as the sheep.

No man in this world can promise himself more hours of life than God is pleased to grant him; because death if deaf, and when he knocks at the door of life is always in a hurry, and will not be detained either by fair means or force, by sceptres or mitres, as the report goes, and as we have often heard it declared from the pulpit.

The hen sits, if it be but upon one egg.

Many littles make a mickle, and he that is getting aught is losing naught.

While there are peas in the dove-cote, it shall never want pigeons.

A good reversion is better than bad possession, and a good claim better than bad pay.

The bread eaten, the company broke up.

A man must be a man, and a woman a woman.

Nothing inspires a knight-errant with so much valor as the favor of his mistress.

O envy! thou root of infinite mischief and canker-worm of virtue! The commission of all other vices, Sancho, is attended with some sort of delight; but envy produces nothing in the heart that harbors it but rage, rancor, and disgust.

The love of fame is one of the most active principles in the human breast.

Let us keep our holy days in peace, and not throw the rope after the bucket.

"And now pray tell me which is the most difficult, to raise a dead man to life or to slay a giant?"

"The answer is very obvious," answered Don Quixote; "to raise a dead man."

"There I have caught you!" quoth Sancho. "Then his fame who raises the dead, gives sight to the blind, makes the lame walk, and cures the sick; who has lamps burning near his grave, and good Christians always in his chapels, adoring his relics upon their knees,—his fame, I say, shall be greater both in this world and the next than that which all the heathen emperors and knights-errant in the world ever had or ever shall have."

"I grant it," answered Don Quixote.

"Then," replied Sancho, "the bodies and relics of saints have this power and grace, and these privileges, or how do you call them, and with the license of our holy mother church have their lamps, winding-sheets, crutches, pictures, perukes, eyes, and legs, whereby they increase people's devotion and spread abroad their own Christian fame. Kings themselves carry the bodies or relics of saints upon their shoulders, kiss the fragments of their bones, and adorn their chapels and most favorite altars with them."

"Certainly, but what wouldst thou infer from all this, Sancho?" quoth Don Quixote.

"What I mean," said Sancho, "is, that we had better turn saints immediately, and we shall then soon get that fame we are seeking after. And pray take notice, sir, that it was but yesterday—I mean very lately—a couple of poor barefooted friars were canonized, and people now reckon it a greater happiness to touch or kiss the iron chains that bound them, and which are now held in greater veneration than Orlando's sword in the armory of our lord the king, Heaven save him; so that it is better to be a poor friar of the meanest order than the bravest knight-errant, because four dozen of good penitent lashes are more esteemed in the sight of God than two thousand tilts with a lance, though it be against giants, goblins, or dragons."

"I confess," answered Don Quixote, "all this is true. We cannot all be friars, and many and various are the ways by which God conducts his elect to Heaven. Chivalry is a kind of religious profession, and some knights are now saints in glory."

"True," quoth Sancho, "but I have heard say there are more friars in Heaven than knights-errant."

"It may well be so," replied Don Quixote, "because their number is much greater than that of knights-errant."

"And yet," quoth Sancho, "there are abundance of the errant sort."

"Abundance, indeed," answered Don Quixote, "but few who deserve the name of knight."

There is a time for jesting, and a time when jokes are unseasonable.

Truth may bend but never break, and will ever rise above falsehood, like oil above water.

With lovers the external actions and gestures are couriers, which bear authentic tidings of what is passing in the interior of the soul.

A stout heart flings misfortune.

Where you meet with no books you need expect no bacon.

The hare often starts where the hunter least expects her.

There is a remedy for everything but death, who will take us in his clutches spite of our teeth.

Show me who thou art with, and I will tell thee what thou art.

Not with whom thou wert bred, but with whom thou art fed.

Sorrow was made for man, not for beasts; yet if men encourage melancholy too much, they become no better than beasts.

"Thou bringest me good news, then?" cried Don Quixote.

"So good," answered Sancho, "that your worship has only to clap spurs to Rozinante, and get out upon the plain, to see the lady Dulcinea del Toboso, who, with a couple of her damsels, is coming to pay your worship a visit."

"Gracious Heaven!" exclaimed Don Quixote, "what dost thou say? Take care that thou beguilest not my real sorrow by a counterfeit joy."

"What should I get," answered Sancho, "by deceiving your worship, only to be found out the next moment? Come, sir, put on, and you will see the princess our mistress all arrayed and adorned—in short, like herself. She and her damsels are one blaze of naming gold; all strings of pearls, all diamonds, all rubies, all cloth of tissue above ten hands deep; their hair loose about their shoulders, like so many sunbeams blowing about in the wind; and what is more, they come mounted upon three pied belfreys, the finest you ever laid eyes on."

"Palfreys, thou wouldst say, Sancho," quoth Don Quixote.

"Well, well," answered Sancho, "belfreys and palfreys are much the same thing; but let them be mounted how they will, they are sure the finest creatures one would wish to see; especially my mistress the princess Dulcinea, who dazzles one's senses."

They were now got out of the wood, and saw the three wenches very near.

Don Quixote looked eagerly along the road towards Toboso, and seeing nobody but the three wenches, he asked Sancho, in much agitation, whether they were out of the city when he left them.

"Out of the city!" answered Sancho; "are your worship's eyes in the nape of your neck, that you do not see them now before you, shining like the sun at noon-day?"

"I see only three country girls," answered Don Quixote, "on three asses."

"Now, Heaven keep me from the devil," answered Sancho; "is it possible that three palfreys, or how do you call them, white as the driven snow, should look to you like asses? As the Lord liveth, you shall pluck off this beard of mine if it be so."

"I tell thee, friend Sancho," answered Don Quixote, "that it is as certain they are asses, as that I am Don Quixote and thou Sancho Panza;—at least, so they seem to me."

"Sir," quoth Sancho, "say not such a thing; but snuff those eyes of yours, and come and pay reverence to the mistress of your soul." So saying he advanced forward to meet the peasant girls, and, alighting from Dapple, he laid hold of one of their asses by the halter, and bending both knees to the ground, said to the girl: "Queen, princess, and duchess of beauty, let your haughtiness and greatness be pleased to receive into grace and good-liking your captive knight, who stands turned there into stone, all disorder, and without any pulse, to find himself before your magnificent presence. I am Sancho Panza, his squire, and he is that way-worn knight Don Quixote de la Mancha, otherwise called the Knight of the Sorrowful Figure."

It is not courage, but rashness, for one man singly to encounter an army, where death is present, and where emperors fight in person, assisted by good and bad angels.

Good Christians should never revenge injuries.

A sparrow in the hand is better than a vulture on the wing.

At the conclusion of this drama of life, death strips us of the robes which make the difference between man and man, and leaves us all on one level in the grave.

From a friend to a friend, etc.

Nor let it be taken amiss that any comparison should be made between the mutual cordiality of animals and that of men; for much useful knowledge and many salutary precepts have been taught by the brute creation.

We may learn gratitude as well as vigilance from cranes, foresight from ants, modesty from elephants, and loyalty from horses.

Harken, and we shall discover his thoughts by his song, for out of the abundance of the heart the mouth speaketh.

sonnet.

Bright authoress of my good or ill,

Prescribe the law I must observe;

My heart, obedient to thy will,

Shall never from its duty swerve.

If you refuse my griefs to know,

The stifled anguish seals my fate;

But if your ears would drink my woe,

Love shall himself the tale relate.

Though contraries my heart compose,

Hard as the diamond's solid frame,

And soft as yielding wax that flows,

To thee, my fair, 'tis still the same.

Take it, for every stamp prepared;

Imprint what characters you choose;

The faithful tablet, soft or hard,

The dear impression ne'er shall lose.

The sorrows that may arise from well-placed affections, ought rather to be accounted blessings than calamities.

Good fare lessens care.

The rarest sporting is that we find at other people's cost.

Covetousness bursts the bag.

Other folk's burdens break the ass's back.

There is no road so smooth but it has its stumbling-places.

Madness will have more followers than discretion.

Comparisons in grief lessen its weight.

If the blind lead the blind, both may fall into the ditch.

A good paymaster needs no pledge.

Nobody knows the heart of his neighbor; some go out for wool and come home shorn.

Let us drink and live, for time takes care to rid us of our lives, without our seeking ways to go before our appointed term and season.

"You must know I have had in my family, by the father's side, two of the rarest tasters that were ever known in La Mancha; and I will give you a proof of their skill. A certain hogshead was given to each of them to taste, and their opinion asked as to the condition, quality, goodness, or badness, of the wine. One tried it with the tip of his tongue; the other only put it to his nose. The first said the wine savored of iron; the second said it had rather a twang of goat's leather. The owner protested that the vessel was clean, and the wine neat, so that it could not taste either of iron or leather. Notwithstanding this, the two famous tasters stood positively to what they had said. Time went on;

the wine was sold off, and, on cleaning the cask, a small key, hanging to a leathern thong, was found at the bottom. Judge then, sir, whether one of that race may not be well entitled to give his opinion in these matters."

"That being the case," quoth he of the wood, "we should leave off seeking adventures, and, since we have a good loaf, let us not look for cheesecakes."

The conquered must be at the discretion of the conqueror.

It is easy to undertake, but more difficult to finish a thing.

"Pray, which is the greater madman, he who is so because he cannot help it, or he who is so on purpose?"

"The difference between these two sorts of madmen is," replied Sampson, "that he who cannot help it will remain so, and he who deliberately plays the fool may leave off when he thinks fit."

Heaven knows the truth of all things.

The ancient sages, who were not enlightened with the knowledge of the true God, reckoned the gifts of fortune and nature, abundance of friends, and increase of dutiful children, as constituting part of the supreme happiness.

Letters without virtue are like pearls on a dunghill.

DON QUIXOTE ON POETRY

Poetry I regard as a tender virgin, young and extremely beautiful, whom divers other virgins—namely, all the other sciences—are assiduous to enrich, to polish, and adorn. She is to be served by them, and they are to be ennobled through her. But the same virgin is not to be rudely handled, nor dragged through the streets, nor exposed in the market-places, nor posted on the corners of gates of palaces. She is of so exquisite a nature that he who knows how to treat her will convert her into gold of the most inestimable value. He who possesses her should guard her with vigilance; neither suffering her to be polluted by obscene, nor degraded by dull and frivolous works. Although she must be in no wise venal, she is not, therefore, to despise the fair reward of honorable labors, either in heroic or dramatic composition. Buffoons must not come near her, neither must she be approached by the ignorant vulgar, who have no sense of her charms; and this term is equally applicable to all ranks, for whoever is ignorant is vulgar. He, therefore, who, with the qualifications I have named, devotes himself to poetry, will be honored and esteemed by all nations distinguished for intellectual cultivation.

Indeed, it is generally said that the gift of poesy is innate—that is, a poet is born a poet, and, thus endowed by Heaven, apparently without study or art, composes things which verify the saying, Est Deus in nobis, etc. Thus the poet of nature, who improves himself by art, rises far above him who is merely the creature of study. Art may improve, but cannot surpass nature; and, therefore, it is the union of both which produces the perfect poet.

Let him direct the shafts of satire against vice, in all its various forms, but not level them at individuals, like some who, rather than not indulge their mischievous wit, will hazard a disgraceful banishment to the Isles of Pontus. If the poet be correct in his morals, his verse will partake of the same purity: the pen is the tongue of the mind, and what his conceptions are, such will be his productions. The wise and virtuous subject who is gifted with a poetic genius is ever honored and enriched by his sovereign, and crowned with the leaves of the tree which the thunderbolt hurts not, as a token that all should respect those brows which are so honorably adorned.

Forewarned, forearmed; to be prepared is half the victory.

It is a nobler sight to behold a knight-errant assisting a widow in solitude than a courtier-knight complimenting a damsel in the city.

Well I know that fortitude is a virtue placed between the two extremes of cowardice and rashness: but it is better the valiant should rise to the extreme of temerity than sink to that of cowardice, for, as it is easier for the prodigal than the miser to become liberal, so it is much easier for the rash than the cowardly to become truly brave.

THE ADVENTURE WITH THE LIONS.

Don Quixote, after having wiped his head, face, beard, and helmet, again put it on, and fixing himself firm in his stirrups, adjusting his sword, and grasping his lance, he exclaimed, "Now, come what may, I am prepared to encounter Satan himself!"

They were soon overtaken by the cart with flags, which was attended only by the driver, who rode upon one of the mules, and a man sitting upon the fore part of it. Don Quixote planted himself just before them, and said, "Whither go ye, brethren? What carriage is this? What does it contain, and what are those banners?"

"The cart is mine," answered the carter, "and in it are two fierce lions, which the general of Oran is sending to court as a present to his majesty; the flags belong to our liege the king, to show that what is in the cart belongs to him."

"And are the lions large?" demanded Don Quixote.

"Larger never came from Africa to Spain," said the man on the front of the cart; "I am their keeper, and in my time have had charge of many lions, but never of any so large as these. They are a male and a female; the male is in the first cage, and the female is in that behind. Not having eaten to-day, they are now hungry and therefore, sir, stand aside, for we must make haste to the place where they are to be fed."

"What!" said Don Quixote, with a scornful smile, "lion-whelps against me! Against me, your puny monsters! and at this time of day! By yon blessed sun! those who sent them hither shall see whether I am a man to be scared by lions. Alight, honest friend! and, since you are their keeper, open the cages and turn out your savages of the desert: for in the midst of this field will I make them know who Don Quixote de la Mancha is, in spite of the enchanters that sent them hither to me."

"So, so," quoth the gentleman to himself, "our good knight has now given us a specimen of what he is; doubtless the curds have softened his skull, and made his brains mellow."

Sancho now coming up to him, "For Heaven's sake, sir," cried he, "hinder my master from meddling with these lions; for if he does they will tear us all to pieces."

"What, then, is your master so mad," answered the gentleman, "that you really fear he will attack such fierce animals?"

"He is not mad," answered Sancho, "but daring."

"I will make him desist," replied the gentleman; and, going up to Don Quixote, who was importuning the keeper to open the cages, "Sir," said he, "Knights-errant should engage in adventures that, at least, afford some prospect of success, and not such as are altogether desperate; for the valor which borders on temerity has in it more of madness than courage. Besides, sir knight, these lions do not come to assail you: they are going to be presented to his majesty; and it is, therefore, improper to detain them or retard their journey."

"Sweet sir," answered Don Quixote, "go hence, and mind your decoy partridge, and your stout ferret, and leave every one to his functions. This is mine, and I shall see whether these gentlemen lions will come against me or not." Then, turning to the keeper, he said, "I vow to Heaven, Don Rascal, if thou dost not instantly open the cages, with this lance I will pin thee to the cart."

The carter seeing that the armed lunatic was resolute, "Good sir," said he, "for charity's sake, be pleased to let me take off my mules and get with them out of danger, before the lions are let loose: for should my cattle be killed, I am undone for ever, as I have no other means of living than by this cart and these mules."

"Incredulous wretch!" cried Don Quixote, "unyoke and do as thou wilt; but thou shalt soon see that thy trouble might have been spared."

The carter alighted and unyoked in great haste. The keeper then said aloud, "Bear witness, all here present, that against my will, and by compulsion, I open the cages and let the lions loose. I protest against what this gentleman is doing, and declare all the mischief done by these beasts shall be placed to his account, with my salary and perquisites over and above. Pray, gentlemen, take care of yourselves before I open the door; for, as to myself, I am sure they will do me no hurt."

Again the gentleman pressed Don Quixote to desist from so mad an action; declaring to him that he was thereby provoking God's wrath. Don Quixote replied that he knew what he was doing. The gentleman rejoined, and entreated him to consider well of it, for he was certainly deceived.

"Nay, sir," replied Don Quixote, "if you will not be a spectator of what you think will prove a tragedy, spur your flea-bitten, and save yourself."

Sancho, too, besought him, with tears in his eyes, to desist from an enterprise compared with which that of the windmills, the dreadful one of the fulling-mills, and in short, all the exploits he had performed in the whole course of his life, were mere tarts and cheesecakes. "Consider, sir," added Sancho, "here is no enchantment, nor anything like it; for I saw, through the grates and chinks of the cage, the paw of a true lion; and I guess, by the size of its claw, that it is bigger than a mountain."

"Thy fears," answered Don Quixote, "would make it appear to thee larger than half the world. Retire, Sancho, and leave me; and if I perish here, thou knowest our old agreement: repair to Dulcinea—I say no more." To these he added other expressions, which showed the firmness of his purpose, and that all argument would be fruitless. The gentleman would fain have compelled him to desist, but thought himself unequally matched in weapons and armor, and that it Would not be prudent to engage with a madman, whose violence and menaces against the keeper were now redoubled; the gentleman therefore spurred his mare, Sancho his Dapple, and the carter his mules, and all endeavored to get as far off as possible from the cart, before the lions were let loose. Sancho bewailed the death of his master; verily believing it would now overtake him between the paws of the lions; he cursed his hard fortune, and the unlucky hour when he again entered into his service. But, notwithstanding his tears and lamentations, he kept urging on his Dapple to get far enough from the cart. The keeper, seeing that the fugitives were at a good distance, repeated his arguments and entreaties, but to no purpose: Don Quixote answered that he heard him, and desired he would trouble himself no more, but immediately obey his commands, and open the door.

Whilst the keeper was unbarring the first gate, Don Quixote deliberated within himself whether it would be best to engage on horseback or not, and finally determined it should be on foot, as Rozinante might be terrified at the sight of the lions. He therefore leaped from his horse, flung aside his lance, braced on his shield, and drew his sword; and marching slowly, with marvellous intrepidity and an undaunted heart, he planted himself before the car, devoutly commending himself, first to God and then to his mistress Dulcinea.

Here it is to be noted that the author of this faithful history, coming to this passage, falls into exclamations, and cries out, O strenuous and beyond all expression courageous Don Quixote de la Mancha! thou mirror wherein all the valiant ones of the world may behold themselves, thou second and new Don Manuel de Leon, who was the glory and honor of the Spanish knights! With what words shall I relate this tremendous exploit? By what arguments shall I render it credible to succeeding ages? or what praises, though above all hyperboles hyperbolical, do not fit and become thee? Thou, alone, on foot, intrepid and magnanimous, with a single sword, and that none of the sharpest, with a shield not of the brightest and most shining steel, standest waiting for and expecting two of the fiercest lions that the forests of Africa ever bred. Let thy own deeds praise thee, valorous Manchegan! for here I must leave off for want of words whereby to enhance them. Here the author ends his exclamation, and resumes the thread of the history, saying:—

The keeper, seeing Don Quixote fixed in his posture, and that he could not avoid letting loose the male lion on pain of falling under the displeasure of the angry and daring knight, set wide open the door of the first cage, where lay the lion, which appeared to be of an extraordinary bigness and of a hideous and frightful aspect. The first thing he did was to turn himself round in the cage, reach out a paw, and stretch himself at full length. Then he gaped and yawned very leisurely; then licked the dust off his eyes, and washed his face, with some half a yard of tongue. This done, he thrust his head out of the cage and stared round on all sides with eyes of fire-coals,—a sight and aspect enough to have struck terror into temerity itself. Don Quixote only observed him with attention, wishing he would leap out from the car and grapple with him, that he might tear him in pieces, to such a pitch of extravagance had his unheard-of madness transported him.

But the generous lion, more civil than arrogant, taking no notice of his vaporing and bravados, after having stared about him, as has been said, turned his back and showed his posteriors to Don Quixote, and with great phlegm and calmness laid himself down again in the cage; which Don Quixote perceiving, he ordered the keeper to give him some blows and provoke him to come forth.

"That I will not do," answered the keeper; "for, should I provoke him, I myself shall be the first he will tear in pieces. Be satisfied, signor cavalier, with what is done, which is all that can be said in point of courage, and do not tempt fortune a second time. The lion has the door open, and it is in his choice to come forth or not; and since he has not yet come out, he will not come out all this day. The greatness of your worship's courage is already sufficiently shown. No brave combatant, as I take it, is obliged to more than to challenge his foe, and expect him in the field; and if the antagonist does not meet him, the disgrace falls on him, while the challenger is entitled to the crown of victory."

"That is true," answered Don Quixote; "shut the door, and give me a certificate in the best form you can of what you have here seen me perform. It should be known that you opened the door to the lion; that I waited for him; that he came not out; again I waited for him; again he came not out; and again he laid himself down. I am bound to no more,—enchantments avaunt! So Heaven prosper right and justice and true chivalry! Shut the door, as I told thee, while I make a signal to the fugitive and absent, that from your own mouth they may have an account of this exploit."

The keeper closed the door, and Don Quixote, having fixed the linen cloth with which he had wiped the curds from his face upon the point of his lance, began to hail the troop in the distance, who, with the gentleman in green at their head, were still retiring, but looking round at every step, when suddenly Sancho observed the signal of the white cloth.

"May I be hanged," cried he, "if my master has not vanquished the wild beasts, for he is calling to us!"

They all stopped, and saw that it was Don Quixote that made the sign; and, their fear in some degree abating, they ventured to return slowly till they could distinctly hear the words of Don Quixote, who continued calling to them. When they had reached the cart again, Don Quixote said to the driver: "Now, friend, put on your mules again, and in Heaven's name proceed; and, Sancho, give two crowns to him and the keeper, to make them amends for this delay."

"That I will, with all my heart," answered Sancho; "but what has become of the lions? are they dead or alive?"

The keeper then very minutely, and with due pauses, gave an account of the conflict, enlarging, to the best of his skill, on the valor of Don Quixote, at sight of whom the daunted lion would not, or durst not, stir out of the cage, though he had held open the door a good while; and, upon his representing to the knight that it was tempting God to provoke the lion, and to force him out, he had at length, very reluctantly, permitted him to close it again.

"What sayest thou to this, Sancho?" said Don Quixote; "can any enchantment prevail against true courage? Enchanters may, indeed, deprive me of good fortune, but of courage and resolution they never can."

Sancho gave the gold crowns; the carter yoked his mules; the keeper thanked Don Quixote for his present, and promised to relate this valorous exploit to the king himself when he arrived at court.

"If, perchance, his majesty," said Don Quixote, "should inquire who performed it, tell him the Knight of the Lions; for henceforward I resolve that the title I have hitherto borne, of the Knight of the Sorrowful Figure, shall be thus changed, converted, and altered; and herein I follow the ancient practice of knights-errant, who changed their names at pleasure."

It is a gallant sight to see a cavalier in shining armor prancing over the lists at some gay tournament in sight of the ladies; it is a gallant sight when, in the middle of a spacious square, a brave cavalier, before the eyes of his prince, transfixes with his lance a furious bull; and a gallant show do all those knights make, who, in military or other exercises, entertain, enliven, and do honor to their prince's court; but far above all these is the knight-errant, who, through deserts and solitudes, through cross-ways, through woods, and over mountains, goes in quest of perilous adventures, which he undertakes and accomplishes only to obtain a glorious and immortal fame.

All knights have their peculiar functions. Let the courtier serve the ladies, adorn his prince's court with rich liveries, entertain the poorer cavaliers at his splendid table, order his jousts, manage tournaments, and show himself great, liberal, and magnificent; above all, a good Christian, and thus will he fulfil his duties.

In enterprises of every kind, it is better to lose the game by a card too much than one too little; for it sounds better to be called rash and daring than timorous and cowardly.

"Signor Don Diego de Miranda, your father, sir, has informed me of the rare talents you possess, and particularly that you are a great poet."

"Certainly not a great poet," replied Lorenzo; "it is true I am fond of poetry, and honor the works of good poets; but I have no claim to the title my father is pleased to confer upon me."

"I do not dislike this modesty," answered Don Quixote; "for poets are usually very arrogant, each thinking himself the greatest in the world."

"There is no rule without an exception," answered Don Lorenzo; "and surely there may be some who do not appear too conscious of their real merits."

"Very few, I believe," said Don Quixote.

THE SCIENCE OF KNIGHT-ERRANTRY

"It is a science," replied Don Quixote, "which comprehends all, or most of the other sciences; for he who professes it must be learned in the law, and understand distributive and commutative justice, that he may know not only how to assign to each man what is truly his own, but what is proper for him to possess; he must be conversant in divinity, in order to be able to explain, clearly and distinctly, the Christian faith which he professes; he must be skilled in medicine, especially in botany, that he may know both how to cure the diseases with which he may be afflicted, and collect the various remedies which Providence has scattered in the midst of the wilderness, nor be compelled on every emergency to be running in quest of a physician to heal him; he must be an astronomer, that he may if necessary ascertain by the stars the exact hour of the night and what part or climate of the world he is in; he must understand mathematics, because he will have occasion for them; and taking it for granted that he must be adorned with all the cardinal and theological virtues, I descend to other more minute particulars, and say that he must know how to swim as well as it is reported of Fish Nicholas; he must know how to shoe a horse and repair his saddle and bridle: and to return to higher concerns, he must preserve his faith inviolable towards Heaven, and also to his mistress; he must be chaste in his thoughts, modest in his words, liberal in good works, valiant in exploits, patient in toils, charitable to the needy, and steadfastly adhering to the truth, even at the hazard of his life. Of all these great and small parts a good knight-errant is composed."

the text.

Could I recall departed joy,

Though barred the hopes of greater gain,

Or now the future hours employ

That must succeed my present pain.

the paraphrase.

All fortune's blessings disappear,
She's fickle as the wind;
And now I find her as severe
As once I thought her kind.
How soon the fleeting pleasures passed!
How long the lingering sorrows last!
Unconstant goddess, in thy haste,
Do not thy prostrate slave destroy,
I'd ne'er complain, but bless my fate,
Could I recall departed joy.
Of all thy gifts I beg but this,
Glut all mankind with more,
Transport them with redoubled bliss,
But only mine restore.
With thought of pleasure once possessed,
I'm now as cursed as I was blessed:
Oh, would the charming hours return,
How pleased I'd live, how free from pain,
I ne'er would pine, I ne'er would mourn.
Though barred the hopes of greater gain.
But oh, the blessing I implore
Not fate itself can give!

Since time elapsed exists no more,
No power can bid it live.
Our days soon vanish into naught,
And have no being but in thought.
Whate'er began must end at last,
In vain we twice would youth enjoy,

In vain would we recall the past,

Or now the future hours employ.

Deceived by hope, and racked by fear,

No longer life can please;

I'll then no more its torments bear,

Since death so soon can ease.

This hour I'll die—but, let me pause—

A rising doubt my courage awes.

Assist, ye powers that rule my fate,

Alarm my thoughts, my rage restrain,

Convince my soul there's yet a state

That must succeed my present pain.

O Flattery, how potent is thy sway! How wide the bounds of thy pleasing jurisdiction!

On the story of Pyramus and Thisbe.

sonnet.

The nymph who Pyramus with love inspired

Pierces the wall, with equal passion fired:

Cupid from distant Cyprus thither flies,

And views the secret breach with laughing eyes.

Here silence, vocal, mutual vows conveys,

And whispering eloquent, their love betrays:

Though chained by fear, their voices dare not pass,

Their souls, transmitted through the chink, embrace.

Ah, woful story of disastrous love!

Ill-fated haste that did their ruin prove!

One death, one grave, unite the faithful pair,

And in one common fame their memories share.

No parents can see the deformity of their own children, and still stronger is this self-deception with respect to the offspring of the mind.

At parting, Don Quixote addressing himself to Don Lorenzo: "I know not," said he, "whether I have already told your worship, but if I have, let me now repeat the intimation, that when you are inclined to take the shortest and easiest road to the inaccessible summit of the temple of fame, you have no more to do, but to leave on one side the path of poetry, which is pretty narrow, and follow that of knight-errantry, which, though the narrowest of all others, will conduct you to the throne of empire in the turning of a straw."

Riches are able to solder abundance of flaws.

Every sheep to its like.

Let every goose a gander choose.

an account of the marriage of camacho the rich; and also the adventure of basilius the poor.

"Come with us, and you will see one of the greatest and richest weddings that has ever been celebrated in La Mancha, or for many leagues round."

"The nuptials of some prince, I presume?" said Don Quixote.

"No," replied the scholar, "only that of a farmer and a country maid: he the wealthiest in this part of the country, and she the most beautiful that eyes ever beheld. The preparations are very uncommon: for the wedding is to be celebrated in a meadow near the village where the bride lives, who is called Quiteria the Fair, and the bridegroom Camacho the Rich: she is about the age of eighteen, and he twenty-two, both equally matched, though some nice folks, who have all the pedigrees of the world in their heads, pretend that the family of Quiteria the Fair has the advantage over that of Camacho; but that is now little regarded, for riches are able to solder up abundance of flaws. In short, this same Camacho is as liberal as a prince; and, intending to be at some cost in this wedding, has taken it into his head to convert a whole meadow into a kind of arbor, shading it so that the sun itself will find some difficulty to visit the green grass beneath. He will also have morris-dances, both with swords and bells; for there are people in the village who jingle and clatter them with great dexterity. As to the number of shoe-clappers invited, it is impossible to count them; but what will give the greatest interest to this wedding is the effect it is expected to have on the slighted Basilius.

"This Basilius is a swain of the same village as Quiteria; his house is next to that of her parents, and separated only by a wall, whence Cupid took occasion to revive the ancient loves of Pyramus and Thisbe: for Basilius was in love with Quiteria from his childhood, and she returned his affection with a thousand modest favors, insomuch that the loves of the two children, Basilius and Quiteria, became the common talk of the village. When they were grown up, the father of Quiteria resolved to forbid Basilius the usual access to his family; and to relieve himself of all fears on his account, he determined to marry his daughter to the rich Camacho; not choosing to bestow her on Basilius, whose endowments are less the gifts of fortune than of nature: in truth he is the most active youth we know; a great pitcher of the bar, an excellent wrestler, a great player at cricket, runs like a buck, leaps like a wild goat, and plays at ninepins as if by witchcraft; sings like a lark, and touches a guitar delightfully and, above all, he handles a sword like the most skilful fencer."

It now began to grow dark, and as they approached the village there appeared before them a new heaven, blazing with innumerable stars. At the same time they heard the sweet and mingled sounds of various instruments—such as flutes, tambourines, psalters, cymbals, drums, and bells; and, drawing still nearer, they perceived a spacious arbor, formed near the entrance into the town, hung round with lights that shone undisturbed by the breeze; for it was so calm that not a leaf was seen to move. The musicians, who are the life and joy of such festivals, paraded in bands up and down this delightful place, some dancing, others singing, and others playing upon different instruments: in short, nothing was there to be seen but mirth and pleasure. Several were employed in raising scaffolds, from which they might commodiously behold the shows and entertainments of the following day, that were to be dedicated to the nuptial ceremony of the rich Camacho and the obsequies of poor Basilius.

If he is poor he cannot think to wed Quiteria. A pleasant fancy, forsooth, for a fellow who has not a groat in his pocket to look for a yoke-mate above the clouds. Faith, sir, in my opinion a poor man should be contented with what he finds, and not be seeking for truffles at the bottom of the sea.

The first thing that presented itself to Sancho's sight was a whole bullock spitted upon a large elm. The fire it was roasted by was composed of a middling mountain of wood, and round it were placed six pots, not cast in common moulds; for they were half-jars, each containing a whole shamble of flesh; and entire sheep were sunk and swallowed up in them, as commodiously as if they were only so many pigeons. The hares ready cased, and the fowls ready plucked, that hung about upon the branches, in order to be buried in the caldrons, were without number. Infinite was the wild fowl and venison hanging about the trees, that the air might cool them. Sancho counted above threescore skins, each of above twenty-four quarts, and all, as appeared afterwards, full of generous wines.

There were also piles of the whitest bread, arranged like heaps of wheat on the threshing-floor, and cheeses, piled up in the manner of bricks, formed a kind of wall. Two caldrons of oil, larger than dyers' vats, stood ready for frying all sorts of batter-ware; and, with a couple of stout peels, they shovelled them up when fried, and forthwith immersed them in a kettle of prepared honey that stood near. The men and women cooks were about fifty in number, all clean, all active, and all in good humor. In the bullock's distended belly were sewed up a dozen sucking pigs, to make it savory and tender. The spices of various kinds, which seemed to have been bought, not by the pound, but by the hundredweight, were deposited in a great chest, and open to every hand. In short the preparation for the wedding was all rustic, but in sufficient abundance to have feasted an army.

Sancho beheld all with wonder and delight. The first that captivated and subdued his inclinations were the flesh-pots, out of which he would have been glad to have filled a moderate pipkin; next the wine-skins drew his affections; and lastly the products of the frying-pans—if such capacious vessels might be so called; and, being unable any longer to abstain, he ventured to approach one of the busy cooks, and in persuasive and hungry terms begged leave to sop a luncheon of bread in one of the pots.

To which the cook answered, "This, friend, is not a day for hunger to be abroad—thanks to rich Camacho. Alight, and look about you for a ladle to skim out a fowl or two, and much good may they do you."

"I see no ladle," answered Sancho.

"Stay," said the cook. "Heaven save me, what a helpless varlet!" So saying, he laid hold of a kettle, and sousing it into one of the half-jars, he fished out three pullets and a couple of geese, and said to Sancho, "Eat, friend, and make your breakfast of this scum, to stay your stomach till dinner-time."

"I have nothing to put it in," answered Sancho.

"Then take ladle and all," quoth the cook; "for Camacho's riches and joy supply everything."

While Sancho was thus employed, Don Quixote stood observing the entrance of a dozen peasants at one side of the spacious arbor, each mounted on a beautiful mare, in rich and gay caparisons, hung round with little bells. They were clad in holiday apparel, and in a regular troop made sundry careers about the meadow, with a joyful Moorish cry of "Long live Camacho and Quiteria! he as rich as she is fair, and she the fairest of the world!"

Don Quixote hearing this, said to himself, "These people, it is plain, have never seen my Dulcinea del Toboso; otherwise they would have been less extravagant in the praise of their Quiteria."

Soon after there entered, on different sides of the arbor, various sets of dancers, among which was one consisting of four-and-twenty sword-dancers; handsome, sprightly swains, all arrayed in fine white linen, and handkerchiefs wrought with several colors of fine silk. One of those mounted on horseback inquired of a young man who led the sword-dance, whether any of his comrades were hurt.

"No," replied the youth; "thank Heaven, as yet we are all well;" and instantly he twined himself in among his companions with so many turns, and so dexterously, that though Don Quixote had often seen such dances before, none had ever pleased him so well. Another dance also delighted him much, performed by twelve damsels, young and beautiful, all clad in green stuff of Cuenza, having their hair partly plaited, and partly flowing, all of golden hue, rivalling the sun itself, and covered with garlands of jessamine, roses and woodbine. They were led up by a venerable old man and an ancient matron, to whom the occasion had given more agility than might have been expected from their years. A Zamora bagpipe regulated their motions, which being no less sprightly and graceful than their looks were modest and maidenly, more lovely dancers were never seen in the world.

A pantomimic dance now succeeded, by eight nymphs, divided into two ranks—"Cupid" leading the one, and "Interest," the other; the former equipped with wings, bow, quiver, and arrows; the latter gorgeously apparelled with rich and variously colored silks, embroidered with gold. The nymphs in Cupid's band displayed their names, written in large letters on their backs. "Poetry" was the first: then succeeded "Discretion," "Good Lineage," and "Valor." The followers of "Interest" were "Liberality," "Bounty," "Wealth," and "Security." This band was preceded by a wooden castle, drawn by savages, clad so naturally in ivy and green cloth, coarse and shaggy, that Sancho was startled. On the front and sides of the edifice was written, "The Castle of Reserve." Four skilful musicians played on the tabor and pipe; Cupid began the dance, and after two movements, he raised his eyes, and bending his bow, pointed an arrow towards a damsel that stood on the battlements of the castle; at the same time addressing to her the following verses:—

cupid's address.

I am the god whose power extends

Through the wide ocean, earth, and sky;

To my soft sway all nature bends,

Compelled by beauty to comply.

Fearless I rule, in calm and storm,

Indulge my pleasure to the full;

Things deemed impossible perform,

Bestow, resume, ordain, annul.

Cupid, having finished his address, shot an arrow over the castle, and retired to his station; upon which Interest stepped forth, and after two similar movements, the music ceasing, he said:—

My power exceeds the might of love,

For Cupid bows to me alone;

Of all things framed by heaven above,

The most respected, sought, and known.

My name is Interest; mine aid

But few obtain, though all desire:

Yet shall thy virtue, beauteous maid,

My constant services acquire.

Interest then withdrew, and Poetry advanced; and, fixing her eyes on the damsel of the castle, she said:—

Let Poetry, whose strain divine

The wondrous power of song displays,

Her heart to thee, fair nymph, consign,

Transported in melodious lays:

If haply thou wilt not refuse

To grant my supplicated boon,

Thy fame shall, wafted by the muse,

Surmount the circle of the moon.

Poetry having retired from the side of Interest, Liberality advanced; and, after making her movements, said:—

My name is Liberality,

Alike beneficent and wise,

To shun wild prodigality,

And sordid avarice despise.

Yet, for thy favor lavish grown,

A prodigal I mean to prove;

An honorable vice I own,

But giving is the test of love.

In this manner all the figures of the two parties advanced and retreated, and each made its movements and recited its verses, some elegant, and some ridiculous of which Don Quixote, who had a very good memory, treasured up the foregoing only.

The bridal pair proceeded towards a theatre on one side of the arbor, decorated with tapestry and garlands, where the nuptial ceremony was to be performed, and whence they were to view the dances and shows prepared for the occasion. Immediately on their arrival at that place, a loud noise was heard at a distance, amidst which a voice was distinguished calling aloud, "Hold a little, rash and thoughtless people!" On turning their heads they saw that these words were uttered by a man who was advancing towards them, clad in a black doublet, welted with flaming crimson. He was crowned with a garland of mournful cypress, and held in his hand a large truncheon; and, as he drew near, all recognized the gallant Basilius, and waited in fearful expectation of some disastrous result from this unseasonable visit.

At length he came up, tired and out of breath, and placed himself just before the betrothed couple; then, pressing his staff, which was pointed with steel, into the ground, he fixed his eyes on Quiteria, and in a broken and tremulous voice thus addressed her: "Ah, false and forgetful Quiteria, well thou knowest that, by the laws of our holy religion, thou canst not marry another man whilst I am living; neither art thou ignorant that, while waiting till time and mine own industry should improve my fortune, I have never failed in the respect due to thy honor. But thou hast cast aside every obligation due to my lawful love, and art going to make another man master of what is mine: a man who is not only enriched, but rendered eminently happy by his wealth; and, in obedience to the will of Heaven, the only impediment to his supreme felicity I will remove, by withdrawing this wretched being. Long live the rich Camacho with the ungrateful Quiteria! Long and happily may they live, and let poor Basilius die, who would have risen to good fortune had not poverty clipped his wings and laid him in an early grave!"

So saying, he plucked his staff from the ground, and, drawing out a short tuck, to which it had served as a scabbard, he fixed what might be called the hilt into the ground, and, with a nimble spring and resolute air, he threw himself on the point, which, instantly appearing at his back, the poor wretch lay stretched on the ground, pierced through and through, and weltering in his blood.

His friends, struck with horror and grief, rushed forward to help him, and Don Quixote, dismounting, hastened also to lend his aid, and taking the dying man in his arms, found that he was still alive. They would have drawn out the tuck, but the priest who was present thought that it should not be done till he had made his confession; as, the moment it was taken out of his body he would certainly expire. But Basilius, not having quite lost the power of utterance, in a faint and doleful voice said: "If, cruel Quiteria, in this my last and fatal agony, thou wouldst give me thy hand, as my spouse, I should hope my rashness might find pardon in heaven, since it procured me the blessing of being thine." Upon which the priest advised him to attend rather to the salvation of his soul than to his bodily appetites, and seriously implore pardon of God for his sins, especially for this last desperate action. Basilius replied that he could not make any confession till Quiteria had given him her hand in marriage as that would be a solace to his mind, and enable him to confess his sins.

Don Quixote, hearing the wounded man's request, said, in a loud voice, that Basilius had made a very just and reasonable request, and, moreover, a very practicable one; and that it would be equally honorable for Signor Camacho to take Quiteria, a widow of the brave Basilius, as if he received her at her father's hand; nothing being required but the simple word, "Yes," which could be of no consequence, since, in these espousals, the nuptial bed must be the grave. Camacho heard all this, and was perplexed and undecided what to do or say; but so much was he importuned by the friends of Basilius to permit Quiteria to give him her hand, and thereby save his soul from perdition, that they at length moved, nay forced him to say that if it pleased Quiteria to give it to him, he should not object, since it was only delaying for a moment the accomplishment of his wishes. They all immediately applied to Quiteria, and, with entreaties, tears, and persuasive arguments, pressed and importuned her to give her hand to Basilius; but she, harder than marble, and more immovable than a statue, returned no answer, until the priest told her that she must decide promptly, as the soul of Basilius was already between his teeth, and there was no time for hesitation.

Then the beautiful Quiteria, in silence, and to all appearance troubled and sad, approached Basilius, whose eyes were already turned in his head, and he breathed short and quick, muttering the name of Quiteria, and giving tokens of dying more like a heathen than a Christian. At last Quiteria, kneeling down by him, made signs to him for his hand. Basilius unclosed his eyes, and fixing them steadfastly upon her, said "O Quiteria! thou relentest at a time when thy pity is a sword to put a final period to this wretched life; for now I have not strength to bear the glory thou conferrest upon me in making me thine, nor will it suspend the pain which shortly will veil my eyes with the dreadful shadow of death. What I beg of thee, O fatal star of mine! is that thou give not thy hand out of compliment, or again to deceive me, but to declare that thou bestowest it upon me as thy lawful husband, without any compulsion on thy will—for it would be cruel in this extremity to deal falsely or impose on him who has been so true to thee."

Here he fainted, and the bystanders thought his soul was just departing. Quiteria, all modesty and bashfulness, taking Basilius's right hand in hers, said: "No force would be sufficient to bias my will; and therefore, with all the freedom I have, I give thee my hand to be thy lawful wife, and receive thine, if it be as freely given, and if the anguish caused by thy rash act doth not trouble and prevent thee."

"Yes, I give it thee," answered Basilius, "neither discomposed nor confused, but with the clearest understanding that Heaven was ever pleased to bestow on me; and so I give and engage myself to be thy husband."

"And I to be thy wife," answered Quiteria, "whether thou livest many years, or art carried from my arms to the grave."

"For one so much wounded," observed Sancho, "this young man talks a great deal. Advise him to leave off his courtship and mind the business of his soul; though to my thinking he has it more on his tongue than between his teeth."

Basilius and Quiteria being thus, with hands joined, the tender-hearted priest, with tears in his eyes, pronounced the benediction upon them, and prayed to Heaven for the repose of the bridegroom's soul; who, as soon as he had received the benediction, suddenly started up, and nimbly drew out the tuck which was sheathed in his body. All the spectators were astonished, and some more simple than the rest cried out "A miracle, a miracle!" But Basilius replied, "no miracle, no miracle, but a stratagem, a stratagem!"

The priest, astonished and confounded, ran to feel, with both his hands, the wound, and found that the sword had passed, not through Basilius's flesh and ribs, but through a hollow iron pipe, cunningly fitted to the place, and filled with blood, so prepared as not to congeal. In short, the priests, Camacho, and the rest of the spectators, found they were imposed upon, and completely duped. The bride showed no signs of regret at the artifice: on the contrary, hearing it said the marriage, as being fraudulent, was not valid, she said that she confirmed it anew; it was, therefore, generally supposed that the matter had been concerted with the privity and concurrence of both parties; which so enraged Camacho and his friends that they immediately had recourse to vengeance, and unsheathing abundance of swords they fell upon Basilius, in whose behalf as many more were instantly drawn, and Don Quixote, leading the van on horseback, his lance upon his arm, and well covered with his shield, made them all give way.

Don Quixote cried aloud, "Hold, sirs, hold! It is not right to avenge the injuries committed against us by love. Remember that the arts of warfare and courtship are in some points alike; in war, stratagems are lawful, so likewise are they in the conflicts and rivalships of love, if the means employed be not dishonorable. Quiteria and Basilius were destined for each other by the just and favoring will of Heaven. Camacho is rich, and may purchase his pleasure when, where and how he pleases. Basilius has but this one ewe-lamb; and no one, however powerful, has a right to take it from him; for those whom God hath joined let no man sunder, and whoever shall attempt it must first pass the point of this lance." Then he brandished it with such vigor and dexterity that he struck terror into all those who did not know him.

Quiteria's disdain made such an impression upon Camacho, that he instantly banished her from his heart. The persuasions, therefore, of the priest, who was a prudent, well-meaning man, had their effect; Camacho and his party sheathed their weapons and remained satisfied, blaming rather the fickleness of Quiteria than the cunning of Basilius. With much reason Camacho thought within himself that if Quiteria loved Basilius when a virgin, she would love him also when married, and that he had more cause to thank Heaven for so fortunate an escape than to repine at the loss he had sustained. The disappointed bridegroom and his followers, being thus consoled and appeased, those of Basilius were so likewise; and the rich Camacho, to show that his mind was free from resentment, would have the diversions and entertainments go on as if they had been really married. The happy pair, however, not choosing to share in them, retired to their own dwelling, accompanied by their joyful adherents; for, if the rich man can draw after him attendants and flatterers, the poor man who is virtuous and deserving is followed by friends who honor and support him.

Don Quixote joined the party of Basilius, having been invited by them as a person of worth and bravery; while Sancho, finding it impossible to remain and share the relishing delights of Camacho's festival, which continued till night, with a heavy heart accompanied his master, leaving behind the flesh-pots of Egypt, the skimmings of which, though now almost consumed, still reminded him of the glorious abundance he had lost.

"If love only were to be considered," said Don Quixote, "parents would no longer have the privilege of judiciously matching their children. Were daughters left to choose for themselves, there are those who would prefer their father's serving-man, or throw themselves away on some fellow they might chance to see in the street, mistaking, perhaps, an impostor and swaggering poltroon for a gentleman, since passion too easily blinds the understanding, so indispensably necessary in deciding on that most important point, matrimony, which is peculiarly exposed to the danger of a mistake, and therefore needs all the caution that human prudence can supply, aided by the particular favor of Heaven. A person who proposes to take a long journey, if he is prudent, before he sets forward will look out for some safe and agreeable companion; and should not he who undertakes a journey for life use the same precaution, especially as his fellow-traveller is to be his companion at bed and board and in all other situations? The wife is not a commodity which, when once bought, you can exchange or return; the marriage bargain, once struck, is irrevocable. It is a noose which, once thrown about the neck, turns to a Gordian knot, and cannot be unloosed till cut asunder by the scythe of death."

By the streets of "by-and-by" one arrives at the house of "never."

God who gives the wound sends the cure.

Nobody knows what is to come. A great many hours come in between this and to-morrow; and in one hour, yea, in one minute, down falls the house. I have seen rain and sunshine at the same moment. A man may go to bed well at night and not be able to stir next morning: and tell me who can boast of having driven a nail in fortune's wheel?

Between the yes and no of a woman I would not undertake to thrust the point of a pin.

"Love, as I have heard say, wears spectacles, through which copper looks like gold, rags like rich apparel, and specks in the eye like pearls."

"A curse on thee, Sancho," said Don Quixote; "what wouldst thou be at? When once thy stringing of proverbs begins, Judas alone—I wish he had thee! —can have patience to the end. Tell me, animal! what knowest thou of nails and wheels, or of anything else?"

"Oh, if I am not understood," replied Sancho, "no wonder that what I say passes for nonsense. But no matter for that,—I understand myself. Neither have I said many foolish things, only your worship is such a cricket."

"Critic, not cricket, fool! thou corrupter of good language!" said the knight.

"Pray, sir, do not be so sharp upon me," answered Sancho, "for I was not bred at court nor studied in Salamanca, to know whether my words have a letter short or one too many. As Heaven shall save me, it is unreasonable to expect that beggarly Sayagnes should talk like Toledans; nay, even some of them are not over-nicely spoken."

Purity, propriety, and elegance of style will always be found among polite, well-bred, and sensible men.

I have heard it said of your fencers that they can thrust you the point of a sword through the eye of a needle.

O happy thou above all that live on the face of the earth, who, neither envying nor envied, canst take thy needful rest with tranquillity of soul, neither persecuted by enchanters nor affrighted by their machinations! Sleep on! a hundred times I say, sleep on! No jealousies on thy lady's account keep thee in perpetual watchings, nor do anxious thoughts of debts unpaid awake thee; nor care how on the morrow thou and thy little straitened family shall be provided for. Ambition disquiets thee not, nor does the vain pomp of the world disturb thee; for thy chief concern is the care of thy ass, since to me is committed the comfort and protection of thine own person,—a burden imposed on the master by nature and custom. The servant sleeps, and the master lies awake considering how he is to maintain, assist, and do him kindness. The pain of seeing the heavens obdurate in withholding the moisture necessary to refresh the earth touches only the master, who is bound to provide in times of sterility and famine for those who served him in the season of fertility and abundance.

So much thou art worth as thou hast, and so much thou hast as thou art worth.

There are only two families in the world,—the have somethings and the have nothings. Nowadays we are apt to feel more often the pulse of property than of wisdom.

An ass with golden trappings makes a better appearance than a horse with a pack-saddle.

"That ought not to be called deception which aims at a virtuous end," said Don Quixote; "and no end is more excellent than the marriage of true lovers; though love," added he, "has its enemies, and none greater than hunger and poverty, for love is all gayety, joy, and content."

SANCHO PANZA ON DEATH.

"In good sooth, signor," said the squire, "there is no trusting to Mrs. Ghostly, I mean Death, who gobbles up the gosling as well as the goose; and, as I have heard our curate observe, tramples down the lofty turrets of the prince as well as the lowly cottage of the swain. That same lady, who is more powerful than coy, knows not what it is to be dainty and squeamish; but eats of everything, and crams her wallet with people of all nations, degrees, and conditions; she is none of your laborers that take their afternoon's nap, but mows at all hours, cutting down the dry stubble as well as the green grass; nor does she seem to chew, but rather swallows and devours everything that falls in her way; for she is gnawed by a dog's hunger that is never satisfied; and though she has no belly, plainly shows herself dropsical, and so thirsty as to drink up the lives of all the people upon earth, just as one would swallow a draught of cool water."

"Enough, friend Sancho," cried the knight, interrupting him in this place; "keep thyself well, now thou art in order, and beware of stumbling again; for really a good preacher could not speak more to the purpose than thou hast spoken upon Death, in thy rustic manner of expression; I say unto thee, Sancho, if thy discretion were equal to thy natural parts, thou mightest ascend the pulpit, and go about teaching and preaching to admiration."

"He is a good preacher who is a good liver," answered Panza, "and that is all the divinity I know."

"And that is sufficient," said the knight; "yet I shall never understand or comprehend, as the fear of God is the beginning of wisdom, how thou, who art more afraid of a lizard than of thy Maker, should be so wise?"

"Signor," replied Sancho, "I desire your worship would determine in your own affairs of chivalry, without taking the trouble to judge of other people's valor or fears; for my own part, I am as pretty a fearer of God as one would desire to see in any neighbor's child; wherefore, I beseech your worship, let me discuss this same scum; for everything else is idle chat, of which we shall be able to give a bad account in the other world."

"The poor man of honor (if a poor man can deserve that title) possesses, in a beautiful wife, a jewel; and when that is taken away, he is deprived of his honor, which is murdered; a beautiful and chaste woman, whose husband is poor, deserves to be crowned with laurel and palms of triumph; for beauty alone attracts the inclinations of those who behold it; just as the royal eagle and soaring hawk stoop to the savory lure; but if that beauty is incumbered by poverty and want, it is likewise attacked by ravens, kites, and other birds of prey; and if she who possesses it firmly withstands all these assaults, she well deserves to be called the crown of her husband.

"Take notice, dearest Basilius," added the knight, "it was the opinion of a certain sage, that there was but one good wife in the whole world; and he advised every husband to believe she had fallen to his share, and accordingly be satisfied with his lot. I myself am not married, nor hitherto have I entertained the least thought of changing my condition; nevertheless, I will venture to advise him who asks my advice, in such a manner, that he may find a woman to his wish; in the first place, I would exhort him to pay more regard to reputation than to fortune; for a virtuous woman does not acquire a good name merely by being virtuous; she must likewise maintain the exteriors of deportment, for the honor of the sex suffers much more from levity and freedom of behavior in public, than from any private misdeeds. If thou bringest a good woman to thy house, it will be an easy task to preserve and even improve her virtue; but, shouldst thou choose a wife of a different character, it will cost thee abundance of pains to mend her; for it is not very practicable to pass from one extreme to another; I do not say it is altogether impossible, though I hold it for a matter of much difficulty."

The ox that is loose is best licked.

Sancho, who had been attentive to the student's discourse, said: "Tell me, sir—so may heaven send you good luck with your books—can you resolve me—but I know you can, since you know every thing—who was the first man that scratched his head? I for my part am of opinion it must have been our father Adam."

"Certainly," answered the scholar; "for there is no doubt but Adam had a head and hair; and, this being granted, he, being the first man in the world, must needs have been the first who scratched his head."

"That is what I think," said Sancho; "but tell me now, who was the first tumbler in the world?"

"Truly, brother," answered the scholar, "I cannot determine that point till I have given it some consideration, which I will surely do when I return to my books, and will satisfy you when we see each other again, for I hope this will not be the last time."

"Look ye, sir," replied Sancho, "be at no trouble about the matter, for I have already hit upon the answer to my question. Know, then, that the first tumbler was Lucifer, when he was cast or thrown headlong from heaven, and came tumbling down to the lowest abyss."

"Sancho," quoth Don Quixote, "thou hast said more than thou art aware of; for some there are who bestow much labor in examining and explaining things which when known are not worth recollecting."

I am thoroughly satisfied that all the pleasures of this life pass away like a shadow or dream, or fade like a flower of the field.

Patience, and shuffle the cards.

We are all bound to respect the aged.

Tell me thy company and I will tell thee what thou art.

Whatever is uncommon appears impossible.

THE BRAYING ALDERMEN

"You must know, gentlemen, that in a town four leagues and a half from this place, a certain alderman happened to lose his ass, all through the artful contrivance (too long to be told) of a wench his maid-servant; and though he tried every means to recover his beast, it was to no purpose. Fifteen days passed, as public fame reports, after the ass was missing, and while the unlucky alderman was standing in the market-place, another alderman of the same town came up to him, and said, 'Pay me for my good news, gossip, for your ass has made its appearance.'

"'Most willingly, neighbor,' answered the other; 'but tell me—where has he been seen?'

"'On the mountain,' answered the other; 'I saw him there this morning, with no panel or furniture upon him of any kind, and so lank that it was grievous to behold him. I would have driven him before me and brought him to you, but he is already become so shy that when I went near him he took to his heels and fled to a distance from me. Now, if you like it we will both go seek him; but first let me put up this of mine at home, and I will return instantly.'

"'You will do me a great favor,' said the owner of the lost ass, 'and I shall be happy at any time to do as much for you.'

"In short the two aldermen, hand in hand and side by side, trudged together up the hill; and on coming to the place where they expected to find the ass, they found him not, nor was he anywhere to be seen, though they made diligent search. Being thus disappointed, the alderman who had seen him said to the other, 'Hark you, friend, I have thought of a stratagem by which we shall certainly discover this animal, even though he had crept into the bowels of the earth, instead of the mountain; and it is this: I can bray marvellously well, and if you can do a little in that way the business is done.'

"'A little, say you, neighbor?' quoth the other, 'before Heaven, in braying I yield to none—no, not to asses themselves.'

"'We shall soon see that,' answered the second alderman; 'go you on one side of the mountain, while I take the other, and let us walk round it, and every now and then you shall bray, and I will bray; and the ass will certainly hear and answer us, if he still remains in these parts.' 'Verily, neighbor, your device is excellent, and worthy your good parts,' said the owner of the ass.

"They then separated, according to agreement, and both began braying at the same instant, with such marvellous truth of imitation that, mutually deceived, each ran towards the other, not doubting but that the ass was found; and, on meeting, the loser said, 'Is it possible, friend, that it was not my ass that brayed?'

"'No, it was I,' answered the other.

"'I declare, then,' said the owner, 'that, as far as regards braying, there is not the least difference between you and an ass; for in my life I never heard anything more natural.'

"'These praises and compliments,' answered the author of the stratagem, 'belong rather to you than to me, friend; for by Him that made me, you could give the odds of two brays to the greatest and most skilful brayer in the world; for your tones are rich, your time correct, your notes well sustained, and cadences abrupt and beautiful; in short, I own myself vanquished, and yield to you the palm in this rare talent.'

"'Truly,' answered the ass owner, 'I shall value and esteem myself the more henceforth, since I am not without some endowment. It is true, I fancy that I brayed indifferently well, yet never flattered myself that I excelled so much as you are pleased to say.'

"'I tell you,' answered the second, 'there are rare abilities often lost to the world, and they are ill-bestowed on those who know not how to employ them to advantage.'

"'Right, brother,' quoth the owner, 'though, except in cases like the present, ours may not turn to much account; and even in this business, Heaven grant it may prove of service.'

"This said, they separated again, to resume their braying; and each time were deceived as before, and met again, till they at length agreed, as a signal, to distinguish their own voices from that of the ass, that they should bray twice together, one immediately after the other. Thus, doubling their brayings, they made the tour of the whole mountain, without having any answer from the stray ass, not even by signs. How, indeed, could the poor creature answer, whom at last they found in a thicket, half devoured by wolves? On seeing the body, the owner said, 'Truly, I wondered at his silence; for, had he not been dead, he certainly would have answered us, or he were no true ass; nevertheless, neighbor, though I have found him dead, my trouble in the search has been well repaid in listening to your exquisite braying.'

"'It is in good hands, friend,' answered the other; 'for if the abbot sings well, the novice comes not far behind him.'

"Hereupon they returned home hoarse and disconsolate, and told their friends and neighbors all that had happened to them in their search after the ass; each of them extolling the other for his excellence in braying. The story spread all over the adjacent villages, and the devil, who sleeps not, as he loves to sow discord wherever he can, raising a bustle in the wind, and mischief out of nothing, so ordered it that all the neighboring villagers, at the sight of any of our towns-people, would immediately begin to bray, as it were hitting us in the teeth with the notable talent of our aldermen. The boys fell to it, which was the same as falling into the hands and mouths of a legion of devils; and thus braying spread far and wide, insomuch that the natives of the town of Bray are as well known and distinguished as the negroes are from white men. And this unhappy jest has been carried so far that our people have often sallied out in arms against their scoffers, and given them battle: neither king nor rook, nor fear nor shame, being able to restrain them. Tomorrow, I believe, or next day, those of our town will take the field against the people of another village about two leagues from us, being one of those which persecute us most: and I have brought the lances and halberds which you saw, that we may be well prepared for them."

The hypocrite who cloaks his knavery is less dangerous to the commonwealth than he who transgresses in the face of day.

He who only wears the garb of piety does less harm than the professed sinner.

I had rather serve the king in his wars abroad, than be the lackey of any beggarly courtier at home.

There is nothing more honorable, next to the service which you owe to God, than to serve your king and natural lord, especially in the profession of arms, which, if less profitable than learning, far exceeds it in glory. More great families, it is true, have been established by learning, yet there is in the martial character a certain splendor, which seems to exalt it far above all other pursuits. But allow me, sir, to offer you a piece of advice, which, believe me, you will find worth your attention. Never suffer your mind to dwell on the adverse events of your life; for the worst that can befall you is death, and when attended with honor there is no event so glorious. Julius Cæsar, that valorous Roman, being asked which was the kind of death to be preferred, "That," said he, "which is sudden and unforeseen!"

Though he answered like a heathen, who knew not the true God, yet, considering human infirmity, it was well said. For, supposing you should be cut off in the very first encounter, either by cannon-shot or the springing of a mine, what does it signify? it is but dying, which is inevitable, and, being over, there it ends. Terence observes that the corpse of a man who is slain in battle looks better than the living soldier who has saved himself by flight; and the good soldier rises in estimation according to the measure of his obedience to those who command him. Observe, moreover, my son, that a soldier had better smell of gunpowder than of musk; and if old age overtakes you in this noble profession, though lame and maimed, and covered with wounds, it will find you also covered with honor; and of such honor as poverty itself cannot deprive you. From poverty, indeed, you are secure; for care is now taken that veteran and disabled soldiers shall not be exposed to want, nor be treated as many do their negro slaves, when old and past service, turning them out of their houses, and, under pretence of giving them freedom, leave them slaves to hunger, from which they can have no relief but in death.

There are often rare abilities lost to the world that are but ill-bestowed on those who do not know how to employ them to advantage.

Who reads and travels much, sees and learns much.

It is the prerogative of God alone to truly comprehend all things. To Him there is nothing past or future. Everything is present.

There is nothing that Time, the discoverer of all things, will not bring to light, even though it be hidden in the bowels of the earth.

Length begets loathing.

Heaven is merciful, and sends relief in the greatest distress.

Affection is the devil.

Heaven help every one to what is their just due, but let us have plain dealing.

When choler once is born,

The tongue all curb doth scorn.

When a brave man flies, he must have discovered foul play.

To retire is not to fly. The valor which has not prudence for its basis is termed rashness, and the successful exploits of the rash are rather to be ascribed to good fortune than to courage.

Other men's pains are easily borne.

He who errs and mends,

Himself to Heaven commends.

Those who sin and kiss the rod,

Find favor in the sight of God.

If you obey the commands of your lord,

You may sit as a guest at his board.

In this world there is nothing but plots and counter-plots, mines and countermines.

A good paymaster needs no surety; and where there is plenty, dinner is soon dressed.

Often the hare starts where she is least expected.

I have heard it said that the power called Nature is like a potter, who, if he can make one beautiful vessel, can in like manner make two, three, ay, and a hundred.

Wit and gay conceits proceed not from dull heads.

Every man must speak of his wants wherever he may be.

Modesty is as becoming a knight-errant as courage.

The master is respected in proportion to the discretion and good breeding of his servants.

Who sets up for a talker and a wit, sinks at the first trip into a contemptible buffoon.

The weapons of gownsmen, like those of women, are their tongues.

Keep company with the good, and you will be one of them.

Not where you were born, but where you were bred.

Well sheltered shall he be

Who leans against a sturdy tree.

An affront must come from a person who not only gives it, but who can maintain it when it is given; an injury may come from any hand.

He who can receive no affront can give none.

One must live long to see much.

He who lives long; must suffer much.

To deprive a knight-errant of his mistress is to rob him of the eyes with which he sees, the sun by which he is enlightened, and the support by which he is maintained. I have many times said, and now I repeat the observation, that a knight-errant without a mistress is like a tree without leaves, a building without cement, and a shadow without the substance by which it is produced.

Possessing beauty without blemish, dignity without pride, love with modesty, politeness springing from courtesy, and courtesy from good breeding, and, finally, of illustrious descent: for the beauty that is of a noble race shines with more splendor than that which is meanly born.

Virtue ennobles blood, and a virtuous person of humble birth is more estimable than a vicious person of rank.

I must inform your graces that Sancho Panza is one of the most pleasant squires that ever served a knight-errant. Sometimes his simplicity is so arch, that to consider whether he is more fool or wag yields abundance of pleasure. He has roguery enough to pass for a knave, and absurdities sufficient to confirm him a fool. He doubts everything and believes everything; and often, when I think he is going to discharge nonsense, he will utter apothegms that will raise him to the skies. In a word, I would not exchange him for any other squire, even with a city to boot; and therefore I am in doubt whether or not it will be expedient to send him to that government which your grace has been so good as to bestow upon him, although I can perceive in him a certain aptitude for such an office; so that, when his understanding is a very little polished, he will agree with any government, like the king with his customs; for we know by repeated experience that great talents and learning are not necessary in a governor, as there are a hundred at least who govern like gerfalcons, though they can hardly read their mother tongue. Provided their intention is righteous and their desire to do justice, they will never want counsellors to direct them in every transaction, like your military governors, who being illiterate themselves, never decide without the advice of an assessor. I shall advise him corruption to eschew, but never quit his due, and inculcate some other small matters that are in my head, which, in process of time, may redound to his own interest as well as to the advantage of the island under his command.

The customs of countries, or of great men's houses, are good as far as they are agreeable.

"Faith, madam," quoth Sancho, "that same scruple is an honest scruple, and need not speak in a whisper, but plain out, or as it lists; for I know it says true, and had I been wise, I should long since have left my master but such is my lot, or such my evil-errantry, I cannot help it,—follow him I must. We are both of the same town; I have eaten his bread; I love him, and he returns my love; he gave me his ass-colts. Above all, I am faithful, so that nothing in the world, can part us but the sexton's spade and shovel; and if your highness does not choose to give me the government you promised, God made me without it, and perhaps it may be all the better for my conscience if I do not get it; for fool as I am, I understand the proverb, 'The pismire had wings to her sorrow;' and perhaps it may be easier for Sancho the squire to get to heaven than for Sancho the governor. They make as good bread here as in France, and by night all cats are gray. Unhappy is he who has not breakfasted at three, and no stomach is a span bigger than another, and may be filled as they say, with straw or with hay.

"Of the little birds in the air, God himself takes the care; and four yards of coarse cloth of Cuenza are warmer than as many of fine Segovia serge; and in travelling from this world to the next, the road is no wider for the prince than the peasant. The Pope's body takes up no more room than that of the sexton, though a loftier person, for in the grave we must pack close together whether we like it or not; so good-night to all.

"And let me tell you again that if your highness will not give me the island because I am a fool, I will be wise enough not to care a fig for it. I have heard say the devil lurks behind the cross; all is not gold that glitters. From the plough-tail Bamba was raised to the throne of Spain, and from his riches and revels was Roderigo cast down to be devoured by serpents, if ancient ballads tell the truth."

None shall dare the loaf to steal

From him that sifts and kneads the meal.

An old dog is not to be coaxed with a crust.

No man is ever a scholar at his birth, and bishops are made of men, not of stones.

There is a Judge in heaven who knows the heart.

A good name is better than tons of gold.

"And you, Signor Panza, be quiet and leave the care of making much of Dapple to me; for being a jewel of Sancho's, I will lay him upon the apple of my eye."

"Let him lie in the stable, my good lady," answered Sancho, "for upon the apple of your grandeur's eye neither he nor I are worthy to lie one single moment,—'slife! they should stick me like a sheep sooner than I would consent to such a thing; for though my master says that, in respect to good manners, we should rather lose the game by a card too much than too little, yet, when the business in hand is about asses and eyes, we should step warily, with compass in hand."

"Carry him, Sancho," quoth the Duchess, "to your government, and there you may regale him as you please, and set him free from further labor."

"Think not, my lady Duchess," quoth Sancho, "that you have said much, for I have seen more asses than one go to governments, and therefore, if I should carry mine, it would be nothing new."

SANCHO'S PLIGHT.

The Duke and Duchess were extremely diverted with the humors of their two guests; and resolving to improve their sport by practising some pleasantries that should have the appearance of a romantic adventure, they contrived to dress up a very choice entertainment from Don Quixote's account of the Cave of Montesinos, taking that subject because the Duchess had observed with astonishment that Sancho now believed his lady Dulcinea was really enchanted, although he himself had been her sole enchanter! Accordingly, after the servants had been well instructed as to their deportment towards Don Quixote, a boar-hunt was proposed, and it was determined to set out in five or six days with a princely train of huntsmen. The knight was presented with a hunting suit proper for the occasion, which, however, he declined, saying that he must soon return to the severe duties of his profession, when, having no sumpters nor wardrobes, such things would be superfluous. But Sancho readily accepted a suit of fine green cloth which was offered to him, intending to sell it the first opportunity.

The appointed day being come, Don Quixote armed himself, and Sancho in his new suit mounted Dapple (which he preferred to a horse that was offered him) and joined the troop of hunters. The Duchess issued forth magnificently attired, and Don Quixote, out of pure politeness, would hold the reins of the palfrey, though the Duke was unwilling to allow it. Having arrived at the proposed scene of their diversion, which was in a wood between two lofty mountains, they posted themselves in places where the toils were to be pitched; and all the party having taken their different stations, the sport began with prodigious noise and clamor, insomuch that between the shouts of the huntsmen, the cry of the hounds, and the sound of the horns, they could not hear each other.

The Duchess alighted, and with a boar-spear in her hand, took her stand in a place where she expected the boars would pass. The Duke and Don Quixote dismounted also, and placed themselves by her side; while Sancho took his station behind them all, with his Dapple, whom he would not quit, lest some mischance should befall him. Scarcely had they ranged themselves in order when a hideous boar of monstrous size rushed out of cover, pursued by the dogs and hunters, and made directly towards them, gnashing his teeth and tossing foam with his mouth.

Don Quixote, on seeing him approach, braced his shield, and drawing his sword, stepped before the rest to meet him. The Duke joined him with his boar-spear, and the Duchess would have been the foremost had not the Duke prevented her. Sancho alone stood aghast, and at the sight of the fierce animal, leaving even his Dapple, ran in terror towards a lofty oak, in which he hoped to be secure; but his hopes were in vain, for, as he was struggling to reach the top, and had got half-way up, unfortunately a branch to which he clung, gave way, and falling with it, he was caught by the stump of another, and here left suspended in the air, so that he could neither get up nor down.

Finding himself in this situation, with his new green coat tearing, and almost in reach of the terrible creature should it chance to come that way, he began to bawl so loud and to call for help so vehemently, that all who heard him and did not see him thought verily he was between the teeth of some wild beast. The tusked boar, however, was soon laid at length by the numerous spears that were levelled at him from all sides, at which time Sancho's cries and lamentations reached the ears of Don Quixote, who, turning round, beheld him hanging from the oak with his head downwards, and close by him stood Dapple, who never forsook him in adversity,—indeed, it was remarked by Cid Hamet, that he seldom saw Sancho Panza without Dapple, or Dapple without Sancho Panza, such was the amity and cordial love that subsisted between them!

Don Quixote hastened to the assistance of his squire, who was no sooner released than he began to examine the rent in his hunting suit, which grieved him to the soul, for he looked upon that suit as a rich inheritance.

The huge animal they had slain was laid across a sumpter-mule, and after covering it with branches of rosemary and myrtle, they carried it, as the spoils of victory, to a large field-tent, erected in the midst of the wood, where a sumptuous entertainment was prepared, worthy of the magnificence of the donor. Sancho, showing the wounds of the torn garments to the Duchess, said: "Had hares or birds been our game, I should not have had this misfortune. For my part I cannot think what pleasure there can be in beating about for a monster that, if it reaches you with a tusk, may be the death of you. There is an old ballad which says,—

"'May fate of Fabila be thine,

And make thee food for bears or swine.'"

"That Fabila," said Don Quixote, "was a king of the Goths, who, going to the chase, was devoured by a bear."

"What I mean," quoth Sancho, "is, that I would not have kings and other great folks run into such dangers merely for pleasure; and, indeed, methinks it ought to be none to kill poor beasts that never meant any harm."

"You are mistaken, Sancho," said the duke, "hunting wild beasts is the most proper exercise for knights and princes. The chase is an image of war: there you have stratagems, artifices, and ambuscades to be employed, in order to overcome your enemy with safety to yourself. There, too, you are often exposed to the extremes of cold and heat; idleness and ease are despised; the body acquires health and vigorous activity: in short, it is an exercise which may be beneficial to many and injurious to none. Besides, it is not a vulgar amusement, but, like hawking, is the peculiar sport of the great. Therefore, Sancho, change your opinion before you become a governor, for then you will find your account in these diversions."

"Not so, i' faith," replied Sancho, "the good governor and the broken leg should keep at home. It would be fine, indeed, for people to come after him about business and find him gadding in the mountains for his pleasure. At that rate what would become of his government? In good truth, sir, hunting and such like pastimes are rather for your idle companions than for governors. The way I mean to divert myself shall be with brag at Easter and at bowls on Sundays and holidays; as for your hunting, it befits neither my condition nor conscience."

"Heaven grant you prove as good as you promise," said the duke, "but saying and doing are often wide apart."

"Be that as it will," replied Sancho, "the good paymaster wants no pawn; and God's help is better than early rising, and the belly carries the legs, and not the legs the belly,—I mean that, with the help of Heaven and a good intention, I warrant I shall govern better than a gos-hawk. Ay, ay, let them put their fingers in my mouth and try whether or not I can bite."

"A curse upon thy proverbs," said Don Quixote, "when will the day come that I shall hear thee utter one coherent sentence without that base intermixture! Let this blockhead alone, I beseech your excellencies, He will grind your souls to death, not between two, but two thousand proverbs, all timed as well and as much to the purpose as I wish God may grant him health, or me, if I desire to hear them."

"Sancho Panza's proverbs," said the duchess, "though more numerous than those of the Greek commentator, are equally admirable for their sententious brevity."

He who has been a good squire will never be a bad governor.

A bad cloak often covers a good drinker.

When a friend drinks one's health, who can be so hard-hearted as not to pledge him?

God's help is better than early rising.

Flame may give light and bonfires may illuminate, yet we may easily be burnt by them; but music is always a sign of feasting and merriment.

the account of the method prescribed to don quixote for disenchanting dulcinea; with other wonderful events.

As the agreeable music approached, they observed that it attended a stately triumphal car, drawn by six gray mules covered with white linen, and upon each of them rode a penitent of light, clothed also in white, and holding a lighted torch in his hand. The car was more than double the size of the others which had passed, and twelve penitents were ranged in order within it, all carrying lighted torches,—a sight which at once caused surprise and terror. Upon an elevated throne sat a nymph, covered with a thousand veils of silver tissue, bespangled with innumerable flowers of gold, so that her dress, if not rich, was gay and glittering. Over her head was thrown a transparent gauze, so thin that through its folds might be seen a most beautiful face; and from the multitude of lights, it was easy to discern that she was young as well as beautiful, for she was evidently under twenty years of age, though not less than seventeen. Close by her sat a figure, clad in a magnificent robe reaching to the feet, having his head covered with a black veil.

The moment this vast machine arrived opposite to where the duke and duchess and Don Quixote stood, the attending music ceased, as well as the harps and lutes within the car. The figure in the gown then stood up, and throwing open the robe and uncovering his face; displayed the ghastly countenance of death, looking so terrific that Don Quixote started, Sancho was struck with terror, and even the duke and duchess seemed to betray some symptoms of fear. This living Death, standing erect, in a dull and drowsy tone and with a sleepy articulation, spoke as follows:—

the enchanter's errand.

Merlin I am, miscalled the devil's son

In lying annals, authorized by time;

Monarch supreme, and great depositary

Of magic art and Zoroastic skill;

Rival of envious ages, that would hide

The glorious deeds of errant cavaliers,

Favored by me and my peculiar charge.

Though vile enchanters, still on mischief bent,

To plague mankind their baleful art employ,

Merlin's soft nature, ever prone to good,

His power inclines to bless the human race.

In Hades' chambers, where my busied ghost

Was forming spells and mystic characters,

Dulcinea's voice, peerless Tobosan maid,

With mournful accents reached my pitying ears;

I knew her woe, her metamorphosed form,

From high-born beauty in a palace graced,

To the loathed features of a cottage wench.

With sympathizing grief I straight revolved

The numerous tomes of my detested art,

And in the hollow of this skeleton

My soul enclosing, hither am I come,

To tell the cure of such uncommon ills.

O glory thou of all that case their limbs

In polished steel and fenceful adamant!

Light, beacon, polar star, and glorious guide

Of all who, starting from the lazy down,

Banish ignoble sleep for the rude toil

And hardy exercise of errant arms!

Spain's boasted pride, La Mancha's matchless knight,

Whose valiant deeds outstrip pursuing fame!

Wouldst thou to beauty's pristine state restore

The enchanted dame, Sancho, thy faithful squire,

Must to his brawny buttocks, bare exposed,

Three thousand and three hundred stripes apply,

Such as may sting and give him smarting pain:

The authors of her change have thus decreed,

And this is Merlin's errand from the shades.

THE PARLEY ABOUT THE PENANCE.

"What!" quoth Sancho, "three thousand lashes! Odd's-flesh! I will as soon give myself three stabs as three single lashes, much less three thousand! The devil take this way of disenchanting! I cannot see what my buttocks have to do with enchantments. Before Heaven! if Signor Merlin can find out no other way to disenchant the lady Dulcinea del Toboso, enchanted she may go to her grave for me!"

"Not lash thyself! thou garlic-eating wretch!" quoth Don Quixote; "I shall take thee to a tree, and tie thee naked as thou wert born, and there, not three thousand and three hundred, but six thousand six hundred lashes will I give thee, and those so well laid on that three thousand three hundred hard tugs shall not tug them off. So answer me not a word, scoundrel! for I will tear thy very soul out!"

"It must not be so," said Merlin; "the lashes that honest Sancho is to receive must not be applied by force, but with his good-will, and at whatever time he pleases, for no term is fixed; and furthermore, he is allowed, if he please, to save himself half the trouble of applying so many lashes, by having half the number laid on by another hand, provided that hand be somewhat heavier than his own."

"Neither another hand nor my own," quoth Sancho, "no hand, either heavy or light, shall touch my flesh. Was the lady Dulcinea brought forth by me that my posteriors must pay for the transgressions of her eyes? My master, indeed, who is part of her, since at every step he is calling her his life, his soul, his support and stay,—he it is who ought to lash himself for her and do all that is needful for her delivery; but for me to whip myself,—no, I pronounce it!"

No sooner had Sancho thus declared himself than the spangled nymph who sat by the side of Merlin arose, and throwing aside her veil, discovered a face of extraordinary beauty; and with a masculine air and no very amiable voice, addressed herself to Sancho: "O wretched squire, with no more soul than a pitcher! thou heart of cork and bowels of flint! hadst thou been required, nose-slitting thief! to throw thyself from some high tower; hadst thou been desired, enemy of human kind! to eat a dozen of toads, two dozen of lizards, and three dozen of snakes; hadst thou been requested to kill thy wife and children with some bloody and sharp scimitar,—no wonder if thou hadst betrayed some squeamishness; but to hesitate about three thousand three hundred lashes, which there is not a wretched school-boy but receives every month, it amazes, stupefies, and affrights the tender bowels of all who hear it, and even of all who shall hereafter be told it. Cast, thou marble-hearted wretch!—cast, I say, those huge goggle eyes upon these lovely balls of mine, that shine like glittering stars, and thou wilt see them weep, drop by drop, and stream after stream, making furrows, tracks, and paths down these beautiful cheeks! Relent, malicious and evil-minded monster! Be moved by my blooming youth, which, though yet in its teens, is pining and withering beneath the vile bark of a peasant wench; and if at this moment I appear otherwise, it is by the special favor of Signor Merlin, here present, hoping that these charms may soften that iron heart, for the tears of afflicted beauty turn rocks into cotton and tigers into lambs. Lash, untamed beast! lash away on that brawny flesh of thine, and rouse from that base sloth which only inclines thee to eat and eat again, and restore to me the delicacy of my skin, the sweetness of my temper, and all the charms of beauty. And if for my sake thou wilt not be mollified into reasonable compliance, let the anguish of that miserable knight stir thee to compassion,—thy master, I mean, whose soul I see sticking crosswise in his throat, not ten inches from his lips, waiting only thy cruel or kind answer either to fly out of his mouth or to return joyfully into his bosom."

Don Quixote, here putting his finger to his throat, "Before Heaven!" said he, "Dulcinea is right, for I here feel my soul sticking in my throat like the stopper of a crossbow!"

"What say you to that, Sancho?" quoth the duchess.

"I say, madam," answered Sancho, "what I have already said, that as to the lashes, I pronounce them."

"Renounce, you should say, Sancho," quoth the duke, "and not pronounce."

"Please your grandeur to let me alone," replied Sancho, "for I cannot stand now to a letter more or less. These lashes so torment me that I know not what I say or do. But I would fain know one thing from the Lady Dulcinea del Toboso, and that is, where she learnt her manner of asking a favor? She comes to desire me to tear my flesh with stripes, and at the same time lays upon me such a bead-roll of ill names that the devil may bear them for me. What! does she think my flesh is made of brass? or that I care a rush whether she is enchanted or not? Where are the presents she has brought to soften me? Instead of a basket of fine linen shirts, night-caps, and socks (though I wear none), here is nothing but abuse. Every one knows that 'the golden load is a burden light;' that 'gifts will make their way through stone walls;' 'pray devoutly and hammer on stoutly;' and 'one take is worth two I'll give thee's.' There's his worship my master, too, instead of wheedling and coaxing me to make myself wool and carded cotton, threatens to tie me naked to a tree and double the dose of stripes. These tender-hearted gentlefolks ought to remember, too, that they not only desire to have a squire whipped, but a governor, making no more of it than saying, 'Drink with your cherries.' Let them learn,—plague take them!—let them learn how to ask and entreat, and mind their breeding. All times are not alike, nor are men always in a humor for all things. At this moment my heart is ready to burst with grief to see this rent in my jacket, and people come to desire that I would also tear my flesh, and that, too, of my own good will. I have just as much mind to the thing as to turn Turk."

"In truth, friend Sancho," said the duke, "if you do not relent and become softer than a ripe fig, you finger no government. It were good indeed, that I should send my islanders a cruel flinty-hearted governor; one who relents not at the tears of afflicted damsels, nor at the entreaties of wise, awful, and ancient enchanters, and sages. In fine, Sancho, either you must whip yourself, or let others whip you, or be no governor."

"My lord," answered Sancho, "may I not be allowed two days to consider what is best for me to do?"

"No, in no wise," quoth Merlin; "here, at this instant and upon this spot, the business must be settled: or Dulcinea must return to Montesinos' cave, and to her former condition of a country wench; or else in her present form be carried to the Elysian fields, where she must wait till the number of lashes be fulfilled."

"Come, honest Sancho," quoth the duchess, "be of good cheer, and show gratitude for the bread you have eaten of your master Don Quixote, whom we are all bound to serve for his good qualities and his high chivalries. Say, yes, son, to this whipping bout, and the devil take the devil, and let the wretched fear; for a good heart breaks bad fortune, as you well know."

"Hark you, Signor Merlin," quoth Sancho, addressing himself to the sage; "pray will you tell me one thing—how comes it about that the devil-courier just now brought a message to my master from Signor Montesinos, saying that he would be here anon, to give directions about this disenchantment; and yet we have seen nothing of them all this while?"

"Pshaw!" replied Merlin, "the devil is an ass and a lying rascal; he was sent from me and not from Montesinos, who is still in his cave contriving, or rather awaiting, the end of his enchantment, for the tail is yet unflayed. If he owes you money, or you have any other business with him, he shall be forthcoming in a trice, when and where you think fit; and therefore come to a decision, and consent to this small penance, from which both your soul and body will receive marvellous benefit; your soul by an act of charity, and your body by a wholesome and timely bloodletting."

"How the world swarms with doctors," quoth Sancho, "the very enchanters seem to be of a trade! Well, since everybody tells me so, though the thing is out of all reason, I promise to give myself the three thousand three hundred lashes, upon condition that I may lay them on whenever I please, without being tied to days or times; and I will endeavor to get out of debt as soon as I possibly can, that the beauty of my lady Dulcinea del Toboso may shine forth to all the world; as it seems she is really beautiful, which I much doubted. Another condition is, that I will not be bound to draw blood, and if some lashes happen only to fly-flap, they shall all go into the account. Moreover if I should mistake in the reckoning, Signor Merlin here, who knows everything, shall give me notice how many I want or have exceeded."

"As for exceedings, there is no need of keeping account of them," answered Merlin; "for when the number is completed, that instant will the lady Dulcinea del Toboso be disenchanted, and come full of gratitude in search of good Sancho, to thank and even reward him for the generous deed. So that no scruples are necessary about surplus and deficiency; and Heaven forbid that I should allow anybody to be cheated of a single hair of their head."

"Go to, then, in God's name," quoth Sancho; "I must submit to my ill fortune: I say I consent to the penance upon the conditions I have mentioned."

No sooner had Sancho pronounced his consent than the innumerable instruments poured forth their music, the volleys of musketry were discharged, while Don Quixote clung about Sancho's neck, giving him, on his forehead and brawny cheeks, a thousand kisses; the duke and duchess, and all who were present, likewise testified their satisfaction. The car now moved on, and in departing the fair Dulcinea bowed her head to the duke and duchess, and made a low curtesy to Sancho.

By this time the cheerful and joyous dawn began to appear, the flowerets of the fields expanded their fragrant beauties to the light; and brooks and streams, in gentle murmurs, ran to pay expecting rivers in their crystal tribute. The earth rejoiced, the sky was clear, and the air serene and calm; all, combined and separately, giving manifest tokens that the day, which followed fast upon Aurora's heels, would be bright and fair. The duke and duchess, having happily executed their ingenious project, returned highly gratified to their castle, and determined on the continuation of fictions which afforded more pleasures than realities.

SANCHO PANZA'S LETTER TO HIS WIFE TERESA PANZA.

If I have been finely lashed, I have been finely mounted up: if I have got a good government, it has cost me many good lashes. This, my dear Teresa, thou canst not understand at present; another time thou wilt.

Thou must know, Teresa, that I am determined that thou shalt ride in thy coach, which is somewhat to the purpose, for all other ways of going are no better than creeping upon all fours, like a cat. Thou shalt be a governor's wife;

see then whether anybody will dare to tread on thy heels. I here send thee a green hunting-suit which my lady duchess gave me; fit it up so that it may serve our daughter for a jacket and petticoat. They say in this country that my master Don Quixote is a sensible madman and a pleasant fool, and that I am not a whit behind him. We have been in Montesino's cave, and the sage Merlin, the wizard, has pitched upon me to disenchant the Lady Dulcinea del Toboso, who among you is called Aldonza Lorenzo. When I have given myself three thousand and three hundred lashes, lacking five, she will be as free from enchantment as the mother that bore her.

Say nothing of this to anybody; for, bring your affairs into council, and one will cry it is white, another it is black. A few days hence I shall go to the government, whither I go with a huge desire to get money; and I am told it is the same with all new governors. I will first see how matters stand, and send thee word whether or not thou shalt come to me.

Dapple is well, and sends thee his hearty service; part with him I will not, though I were made the great Turk. The duchess, my mistress, kisses thy hands a thousand times over. Return her two thousand; for, as my master says, nothing is cheaper than civil words. God has not been pleased to throw in my way another portmanteau and another hundred crowns, as once before; but take no heed, my dear Teresa, for he that has the game in his hand need not mind the loss of a trick,—the government will make up for all. One thing only troubles me: I am told if I once try it I shall eat my very fingers after it; and if so, it will not be much of a bargain, though, indeed, the crippled and maimed enjoy a petty canonry in the alms they receive; so that, one way or another, thou art sure to be rich and happy. God send it may be so, as He easily can, and keep me for thy sake.

Thy husband, the governor,

Sancho Panza.

From this Castle, the 20th of July, 1614.

THE KNIGHT REPROVED.

After a thousand courtly compliments mutually interchanged, Don Quixote advanced towards the table, between the duke and duchess, and, on preparing to seat themselves, they offered the upper end to Don Quixote, who would have declined it but for the pressing importunities of the duke. The ecclesiastic seated himself opposite to the knight, and the duke and duchess on each side.

Sancho was present all the while, in amazement to see the honor paid by those great people to his master; and, whilst the numerous entreaties and ceremonies were passing between the duke and Don Quixote, before he would sit down at the head of the table, he said: "With your honor's leave I will tell you a story of what happened in our town about seats."

Don Quixote immediately began to tremble, not doubting that he was going to say something absurd. Sancho observed him, and, understanding his looks, he said: "Be not afraid, sir, of my breaking loose or saying anything that is not pat to the purpose. I have not forgotten the advice your worship gave me awhile ago about talking much or little, well or ill."

"I remember nothing, Sancho," answered Don Quixote; "say what thou wilt, so as thou sayst it quickly."

"What I would say," quoth Sancho, "is very true, for my master, Don Quixote, who is present, will not suffer me to lie."

"Lie as much as thou wilt for me, Sancho," replied Don Quixote, "I shall not hinder thee; but take heed what thou art going to say."

"I have heeded it over and over again, so that it is as safe as if I had the game in my hand, as you shall presently see."

"Your graces will do well," said Don Quixote, "to order this blockhead to retire, that you may get rid of his troublesome folly."

"By the life of the duke," quoth the duchess, "Sancho shall not stir a jot from me. I have a great regard for him, and am assured of his discretion."

"Many happy years may your holiness live," quoth Sancho, "for the good opinion you have of me, little as I deserve it. But the tale I would tell is this—

"A certain gentleman of our town, very rich and of a good family,—for he was descended from the Alamos of Medina del Campo, and married Donna Mencia de Quinnones, who was daughter to Don Alonzo de Maranon, knight of the order of St. James, the same that was drowned in the Herradura, about whom that quarrel happened in our town, in which it was said my master Don Quixote had a hand, and Tommy the mad-cap, son of Balvastro the blacksmith, was hurt. Pray, good master of mine, is not all this true? Speak, I beseech you, that their worships may not take me for some lying prater."

"As yet," said the ecclesiastic, "I take you rather for a prater than for a liar; but I know not what I shall next take you for."

"Thou hast produced so many witnesses and so many proofs," said Don Quixote, "that I cannot but say thou mayst probably be speaking truth; but, for Heaven's sake, shorten thy story, or it will last these two days."

"He shall shorten nothing," quoth the duchess; "and to please me, he shall tell it his own way, although he were not to finish these six days; and, should it last so long, they would be to me days of delight."

"I must tell you, then," proceeded Sancho, "that this same gentleman—whom I know as well as I do my right hand from my left, for it is not a bow-shot from my house to his—invited a husbandman to dine with him,—a poor man, but mainly honest."

"On, friend," said the chaplain, "for, at the rate you proceed, your tale will not reach its end till you reach the other world."

"I shall stop," replied Sancho, "before I get half-way thither, if it please Heaven! This same farmer coming to the house of the gentleman his inviter—God rest his soul, for he is dead and gone; and, moreover, died like an angel, as it is said,—for I was not by myself, being at that time gone a reaping to Tembleque."

"Prithee, son," said the ecclesiastic, "come back quickly from Tembleque, and stay not to bury the gentleman, unless you are determined upon more burials. Pray make an end of your tale."

"The business, then," quoth Sancho, "was this, that, they being ready to sit down to table,—methinks I see them plainer than ever."

The duke and duchess were highly diverted at the impatience of the good ecclesiastic, and at the length and pauses of Sancho's tale; but Don Quixote was almost suffocated with rage and vexation.

"I say, then," quoth Sancho, "that, as they were both standing before the dinner-table, just ready to sit down, the farmer insisted that the gentleman should take the upper end of the table, and the gentleman as positively pressed the farmer to take it, saying he ought to be master in his own house. But the countryman, piquing himself upon his good breeding, still refused to comply, till the gentleman, losing all patience, laid both his hands upon the farmer's shoulders, and made him sit down by main force, saying, 'Sit thee down, clod-pole! for in whatever place I am seated, that is the upper end to thee.' That is my tale, and truly I think it comes in here pretty much to the purpose."

All things are not alike, nor are men always in a humor for all things.

Leave fear to the cowardly.

A stout heart quails misfortune.

Letters written in blood cannot be disputed.

If you seek advice about your own concerns, one will say it is white and another will swear it is black.

Nothing is so reasonable and cheap as good manners.

He is safe who has good cards to play.

Avarice bursts the bag, and the covetous governor doeth ungoverned justice.

The law's measure

Is the king's pleasure.

The game is as often lost by a card too many as one too few; but a word to the wise is sufficient.

Come, death, with gently-stealing pace,

And take me unperceived away,

Nor let me see thy wished-for face,

Lest joy my fleeting life should stay.

The tyrant fair whose beauty sent

The throbbing mischief to my heart,

The more my anguish to augment,

Forbids me to reveal the smart.

When a thing is once begun, it is almost half finished.

When the heifer you receive,

Have a halter in your sleeve.

Delay breeds danger.

Who sits in the saddle must get up first.

There is nothing so sweet as to command and be obeyed.

It is a pleasant thing to govern, even though it be but a flock of sheep.

instructions which don quixote gave to sancho panza before he went to his government; with other well considered matters.

The duke and duchess being so well pleased with the afflicted duenna, were encouraged to proceed with other projects, seeing that there was nothing too extravagant for the credulity of the knight and squire. The necessary orders were accordingly issued to their servants and vassals with regard to their behavior towards Sancho in his government of the promised island. The day after the flight of Clavileno, the duke bade Sancho prepare, and get himself in readiness to assume his office, for his islanders were already wishing for him as for rain in May. Sancho made a low bow, and said: "Ever since my journey to heaven, when I looked down and saw the earth so very small, my desire to be a governor has partly cooled: for what mighty matter is it to command on a spot no bigger than a grain of mustard-seed; where is the majesty and pomp of governing half a dozen creatures no bigger than hazel-nuts? If your lordship will be pleased to offer me some small portion of heaven, though it be but half a league, I would jump at it sooner than for the largest island in the world."

"Look you, friend Sancho," answered the duke, "I can give away no part of heaven, not even a nail's breadth; for God has reserved to Himself the disposal of such favors: but what it is in my power to give, I give you with all my heart; and the island I now present to you is ready made, round and sound, well-proportioned, and above measure fruitful, and where, by good management, you may yourself, with the riches of the earth, purchase an inheritance in heaven."

"Well, then," answered Sancho, "let this island be forthcoming, and it shall go hard with me but I will be such a governor that, in spite of rogues, heaven will take me in. Nor is it out of covetousness that I forsake my humble cottage and aspire to greater things, but the desire I have to taste what it is to be a governor."

"If once you taste it, Sancho," quoth the duke, "you will lick your fingers after it; so sweet it is to command and be obeyed. And certain I am, when your master becomes an emperor, of which there is no doubt, as matters proceed so well, it would be impossible to wrest his power from him, and his only regret will be that he had it not sooner."

"Faith, sir, you are in the right," quoth Sancho, "it is pleasant to govern, though it be but a flock of sheep."

"Let me be buried with you, Sancho," replied the duke, "if you know not something of every thing, and I doubt not you will prove a pearl of a governor. But enough of this for the present: to-morrow you surely depart for your island, and this evening you shall be fitted with suitable apparel and with all things necessary for your appointment."

"Clothe me as you will," said Sancho, "I shall still be Sancho Panza."

"That is true," said the duke; "but the garb should always be suitable to the office and rank of the wearer: for a lawyer to be habited like a soldier, or a soldier like a priest, would be preposterous; and you; Sancho, must be clad partly like a scholar and partly like a soldier; as, in the office you will hold, arms and learning are united."

"As for learning," replied Sancho, "I have not much of that, for I hardly know my A B C; but to be a good governor, it will be enough that I am able to make my Christ-cross; and as to arms, I shall handle such as are given me till I fall, and so God help me."

"With so good an intention," quoth the duke, "Sancho cannot do wrong."

Here they were joined by Don Quixote, who understanding the subject of their conversation, and the short space allotted to Sancho to prepare for his departure, took the squire by the hand, with the duke's permission, and led him to his apartment, in order to instruct him how to behave in his office. Having entered the chamber he locked the door, and obliging Sancho to sit down by him, spoke to this effect, in a grave and solemn tone:—

"I return infinite thanks to Heaven, friend Sancho, for having ordained that, before I myself have met with the least success, good fortune hath gone forth to bid thee welcome. I, who had balanced the remuneration of thy service in my own prosperity, find myself in the very rudiments of promotion; while thou, before thy time, and contrary to all the laws of reasonable progression, findest thy desire accomplished: other people bribe, solicit, importune, attend levees, entreat, and persevere, without obtaining their suit; and another comes, who, without knowing why or wherefore, finds himself in possession of that office to which so many people laid claim: and here the old saying is aptly introduced, 'A pound of good luck is worth a ton of merit.' Thou, who, in comparison to me, art doubtless an ignorant dunce, without rising early or sitting up late, or, indeed, exerting the least industry: without any pretension more or less than that of being breathed upon by knight-errantry, seest thyself created governor of an island as if it was a matter of moonshine.

"All this I observe, O Sancho, that thou mayst not attribute thy success to thy own deserts: but give thanks to heaven for having disposed matters so beneficially in thy behalf, and then make thy acknowledgments to that grandeur which centres in the profession of knight-errantry. Thy heart being thus predisposed to believe what I have said, be attentive, O my son, to me who am thy Cato, thy counsellor, thy north-pole and guide, to conduct thee into a secure harbor from the tempestuous sea into which thou art going to be engulfed; for great posts and offices of state are no other than a profound gulf of confusion.

"In the first place, O my son, you are to fear God: the fear of God is the beginning of wisdom; and if you are wise you cannot err.

"Secondly, you must always remember who you are, and endeavor to know yourself,—a study of all others the most difficult. This self-knowledge will hinder you from blowing yourself up like the frog in order to rival the size of the ox: if, therefore, you succeed in this learning, the consideration of thy having been a swineherd will, like the peacock's ugly feet, be a check upon thy folly and pride."

"I own I once took care of hogs when I was a boy," said Sancho; "but, after I grew up, I quitted that employment and took care of geese; but I apprehend that matter is not of great consequence, for all governors are not descended from the kingly race."

"No, sure," answered the knight; "and, for that reason, those who are not of noble extraction ought to sweeten the gravity of their function with mildness and affability: which, being prudently conducted, will screen them from those malicious murmurs that no station can escape.

"Conceal not the meanness of thy family, nor think it disgraceful to be descended from peasants; for, when it is seen that thou art not thyself ashamed, none will endeavor to make thee so; and deem it more meritorious to be a virtuous humble man than a lofty sinner. Infinite is the number of those who, born of low extraction, have risen to the highest dignities both in church and state; and of this truth I could tire thee with examples.

"If thou takest virtue for the rule of life, and valuest thyself upon acting in all things conformably thereto, thou wilt have no cause to envy lords and princes; for blood is inherited, but virtue is a common property and may be acquired by all. It has, moreover, an intrinsic worth which blood has not. This being so, if, peradventure, any one of thy kindred visit thee in thy government, do not slight nor affront him; but receive, cherish, and make much of him, for in so doing thou wilt please God, who allows none of His creatures to be despised; and thou wilt also manifest therein a well-disposed nature.

"If thou takest thy wife with thee (and it is not well for those who are appointed to governments to be long separated from their families), teach, instruct, and polish her from her natural rudeness; for it often happens that all the consideration a wise governor can acquire is lost by an ill-bred and foolish woman.

"If thou shouldst become a widower (an event which is possible), and thy station entitles thee to a better match, seek not one to serve thee for a hook and angling-rod, or a friar's hood to receive alms in; for, believe me, whatever the judge's wife receives, the husband must account for at the general judgment, and shall be made to pay fourfold for all that of which he has rendered no account during his life.

"Be not under the dominion of thine own will: it is the vice of the ignorant, who vainly presume on their own understanding.

"Let the tears of the poor find more compassion, but not more justice, from thee than the applications of the wealthy.

"Be equally solicitous to sift out the truth amidst the presents and promises of the rich and the sighs and entreaties of the poor.

"Whenever equity may justly temper the rigor of the law, let not the whole force of it bear upon the delinquent; for it is better that a judge should lean on the side of compassion than severity.

"If, perchance, the scales of justice be not correctly balanced, let the error be imputable to pity, not to gold.

"If, perchance, the cause of thine enemy come before thee, forget thy injuries, and think only on the merits of the case.

"Let not private affection blind thee in another man's cause; for the errors thou shalt thereby commit are often without remedy, and at the expense both of thy reputation and fortune.

"When a beautiful woman comes before thee to demand justice, consider maturely the nature of her claim, without regarding either her tears or her sighs, unless thou wouldst expose thy judgment to the danger of being lost in the one, and thy integrity in the other.

"Revile not with words him whom thou hast to correct with deeds; the punishment which the unhappy wretch is doomed to suffer is sufficient, without the addition of abusive language.

"When the criminal stands before thee, recollect the frail and depraved nature of man, and as much as thou canst, without injustice to the suffering party, show pity and clemency; for, though the attributes of God are all equally adorable, yet His mercy is more shining and attractive in our eyes, and strikes with greater lustre, than His justice.

"If you observe, and conduct yourself by these rules and precepts, Sancho, your days will be long upon the face of the earth; your fame will be eternal, your reward complete, and your felicity unutterable; your children will be married according to your wish; they and their descendants will enjoy titles; you shall live in peace and friendship with all mankind; when your course of life is run, death will overtake you in a happy and mature old age, and your eyes will be shut by the tender and delicate hands of your posterity, in the third or fourth generation.

"The remarks I have hitherto made are documents touching the decoration of your soul; and now you will listen to the directions I have to give concerning thy person and deportment."

OF THE SECOND SERIES OF INSTRUCTIONS DON QUIXOTE GAVE TO SANCHO PANZA

Who that has duly considered Don Quixote's instructions to his squire would not have taken him for a person of singular intelligence and discretion? But, in truth, as it has often been said in the progress of this great history, he raved only on the subject of chivalry; on all others he manifested a sound and discriminating understanding; wherefore his judgment and his actions appeared continually at variance. But, in these second instructions given to Sancho, which showed much ingenuity, his wisdom and frenzy are both singularly conspicuous.

During the whole of this private conference, Sancho listened to his master with great attention, and endeavored so to register his counsel in his mind that he might thereby be enabled to bear the burden of government and acquit himself honorably. Don Quixote now proceeded:—

"As to the regulation of thine own person and domestic concerns," said he, "in the first place, Sancho, I enjoin thee to be cleanly in all things. Keep the nails of thy fingers constantly and neatly pared, nor suffer them to grow as some do, who ignorantly imagine that long nails beautify the hand, and account the excess of that excrement simply a finger-nail, whereas it is rather the talon of the lizard-hunting kestrel,—a foul and unsightly object. A slovenly dress betokens a careless mind; or, as in the case of Julius Cæsar, it may be attributed to cunning.

"Examine prudently the income of thy office, and if it will afford thee to give liveries to thy servants, give them such as are decent and lasting, rather than gaudy and modish; and what thou shalt thus save in thy servants bestow on the poor; so shalt thou have attendants both in heaven and earth—a provision which our vain-glorious great never think of.

"Eat neither garlic nor onions, lest the smell betray thy rusticity. Walk with gravity, and speak deliberately, but not so as to seem to be listening to thyself; for affectation is odious.

"Eat little at dinner and less at supper; for the health of the whole body is tempered in the laboratory of the stomach.

"Drink with moderation; for inebriety never keeps a secret nor performs a promise.

"In the next place, Sancho, do not intermix in thy discourse such a multitude of proverbs as thou wert wont to do; for though proverbs are concise and pithy sentences, thou dost so often drag them in by the head and shoulders that they look more like the ravings of distraction than well-chosen apothegms."

"That defect God himself must remedy," said Sancho; "for I have more proverbs by heart than would be sufficient to fill a large book; and, when I speak, they crowd together in such a manner as to quarrel for utterance; so that my tongue discharges them just as they happen to be in the way, whether they are or are not to the purpose: but I will take care henceforward to throw out those that may be suitable to the gravity of my office: for, 'Where there's plenty of meat, the supper will soon be complete;' 'He that shuffles does not cut;' 'A good hand makes a short game;' and, 'It requires a good brain to know when to give and retain.'"

"Courage, Sancho," cried Don Quixote; "squeeze, tack, and string your proverbs together; here are none to oppose you. My mother whips me, and I whip the top. Here am I exhorting thee to suppress thy proverbs, and in an instant thou hast spewed forth a whole litany of them, which are as foreign from the subject as an old ballad. Remember, Sancho, I do not say that a proverb properly applied is amiss; but, to throw in, and string together old saws helter-skelter, renders conversation altogether mean and despicable.

"When you appear on horseback do not lean backward over the saddle, nor stretch out your legs stiffly from the horse's belly, nor let them hang dangling in a slovenly manner, as if you were upon the back of Dapple; for some ride like jockeys, and some like gentlemen.

"Be very moderate in sleeping; for he who does not rise with the sun cannot enjoy the day; and observe, O Sancho, industry is the mother of prosperity; and laziness, her opposite, never saw the accomplishment of a good wish.

"This is all the advice, friend Sancho, that occurs to me at present; hereafter, as occasions offer, my instructions will be ready, provided thou art mindful to inform me of the state of thy affairs."

"Sir," answered Sancho, "I see very well that all your worship has told me is wholesome and profitable; but what shall I be the better for it if I cannot keep it in my head? It is true, I shall not easily forget what you have said about paring my nails, and marrying again if the opportunity offers; but for your other quirks and quillets, I protest they have already gone out of my head as clean as last year's clouds; and therefore, let me have them in writing; for though I cannot read them myself, I will give them to my confessor, that he may repeat and drive them into me in time of need."

"Heaven defend me!" said Don Quixote, "how scurvy doth it look in a governor to be unable to read or write! Indeed, Sancho, I must needs tell thee that when a man has not been taught to read, or is left-handed, it argues that his parentage was very low, or that, in early life, he was so indocile and perverse that his teachers could beat nothing good into him. Truly this is a great defect in thee, and therefore I would have thee learn to write, even if it were only thy name."

"That I can do already," quoth Sancho; "for when I was steward of the brotherhood in our village, I learned to make certain marks like those upon wool-packs, which they told me, stood for my name. But, at the worst, I can feign a lameness in my right hand, and get another to sign for me: there is a remedy for every thing but death; and, having the staff in my hand, I can do what I please. Besides, as your worship knows, he whose father is mayor — and I, being governor, am, I trow, something more than mayor.

"Ay, ay, let them come that list, and play at bo-peep—ay, fleer and backbite me; but they may come for wool and go back shorn: 'His home is savory whom God loves;'—besides, 'The rich man's blunders pass current for wise maxims;' so that I, being a governor, and therefore wealthy, and bountiful to boot—as I intend to be—nobody will see any blemish in me. No, no, let the clown daub himself with honey, and he will never want flies. 'As much as you have, just so much you are worth,' said my grandam; revenge yourself upon the rich who can."

"Heaven confound thee!" exclaimed Don Quixote; "sixty thousand devils take thee and thy proverbs! This hour, or more, thou hast been stringing thy musty wares, poisoning and torturing me without mercy. Take my word for it, these proverbs will one day bring thee to the gallows;—they will surely provoke thy people to rebellion! Where dost thou find them? How shouldst thou apply them, idiot? for I toil and sweat as if I were delving the ground to utter but one, and apply it properly."

"Before Heaven, master of mine," replied Sancho, "your worship complains of very trifles. Why, in the devil's name, are you angry that I make use of my own goods? for other stock I have none, nor any stock but proverbs upon proverbs; and just now I have four ready to pop out, all pat and fitting as pears in a pannier—but I am dumb: Silence is my name."

"Then art thou vilely miscalled," quoth Don Quixote, "being an eternal babbler. Nevertheless, I would fain know these four proverbs that come so pat to the purpose; for I have been rummaging my own memory, which is no bad one, but for the soul of me, I can find none."

"Can there be better," quoth Sancho, "than—'Never venture your fingers between two eye-teeth;' and with 'Get out of my house—what would you have with my wife?' there is no arguing; and, 'Whether the pitcher hits the stone, or the stone hits the pitcher, it goes ill with the pitcher.' All these, your worship must see, fit to a hair. Let no one meddle with the governor or his deputy, or he will come off the worst, like him who claps his finger between two eye-teeth, and though they were not eye-teeth, 'tis enough if they be but teeth. To what a governor says there is no replying, any more than to 'Get out of my house—what business have you with my wife?' Then as to the stone and the pitcher—a blind man may see that. So he who points to the mote in another man's eye, should first look to the beam in his own, that it may not be said of him, the dead woman was afraid of her that was flayed. Besides, your worship knows well that the fool knows more in his own house than the wise in that of another."

"Not so, Sancho," answered Don Quixote, "the fool knows nothing, either in his own or any other house; for knowledge is not to be erected upon so bad a foundation as folly. But here let it rest, Sancho, for, if thou governest ill, though the fault will be thine, the shame will be mine. However, I am comforted in having given thee the best counsel in my power; and therein having done my duty, I am acquitted both of my obligation and promise; so God speed thee, Sancho, and govern thee in thy government, and deliver me from the fears I entertain that thou wilt turn the whole island topsy-turvy!—which, indeed, I might prevent by letting the duke know what thou art, and telling him that all that paunch-gut and little carcass of thine is nothing but a sack full of proverbs and impertinence."

"Signor," replied Sancho, "if your worship really thinks I am not qualified for that government, I renounce it from henceforward forever, amen. I have a greater regard for a nail's breadth of my soul than my whole body; and I can subsist, as bare Sancho, upon a crust of bread and an onion, as well as governor on capons and partridges; for, while we sleep, great and small, rich and poor, are equal all. If your worship will consider, your worship will find that you yourself put this scheme of government into my head. As for my own part, I know no more of the matter than a bustard; and, if you think the governorship will be the means of my going to the devil, I would much rather go as simple Sancho to Heaven than as a governor to hell-fire."

"Before God!" cried the knight, "from these last reflections thou hast uttered, I pronounce thee worthy to govern a thousand islands. Thou hast an excellent natural disposition, without which all science is naught. Recommend thyself to God, and endeavor to avoid errors in the first intention. I mean, let thy intention and unshaken purpose be to deal righteously in all thy transactions, for Heaven always favors the upright design. And now let us go in to dinner, for I believe their graces wait for us."

Without discretion there can be no wit.

O poverty, poverty! I know not what should induce the great Cordovan poet to call thee a holy, unrequited gift. I, though a Moor, am very sensible, from my correspondence with Christians, that holiness consists in charity, humility, faith, poverty, and obedience; yet, nevertheless, I will affirm that he must be holy indeed, who can sit down content with poverty, unless we mean that kind of poverty to which one of the greatest saints alludes, when he says,

"Possess of all things as not possessing them;" and this is called spiritual poverty. But thou second poverty, which is the cause I spoke of, why wouldst thou assault gentlemen of birth rather than any other class of people? Why dost thou compel them to cobble their shoes, and wear upon their coats one button of silk, another of hair, and a third of glass? Why must their ruffs be generally yellow and ill-starched? (By the by, from this circumstance we learn the antiquity of ruffs and starch. But thus he proceeds:) O wretched man of noble pedigree! who is obliged to administer cordials to his honor, in the midst of hunger and solitude, by playing the hypocrite with a toothpick, which he affects to use in the street, though he has eat nothing to require that act of cleanliness. Wretched he, I say, whose honor is ever apt to be startled, and thinks that everybody at a league's distance observes the patch upon his shoe, his greasy hat, and his threadbare cloak, and even the hunger that consumes him.

Better a blush on the face than a stain in the heart.

Look not in last year's nests for this year's birds.

A SERENADE

And he forthwith imagined that some damsel belonging to the duchess had become enamored of him. Though somewhat fearful of the beautiful foe, he resolved to fortify his heart, and on no account to yield; so, commending himself with fervent devotion to his mistress, Dulcinea del Toboso, he determined to listen to the music; and to let the damsel know he was there he gave a feigned sneeze, at which they were not a little pleased, as they desired above all things that he should hear them. The harp being now tuned, Altisidora began the following song:—

Wake, sir knight, now love's invading,

Sleep in Holland sheets no more;

When a nymph is serenading,

'Tis an arrant shame to snore.

Hear a damsel tall and tender,

Moaning in most rueful guise,

With heart almost burned to cinder

By the sunbeams of thine eyes.

To free damsels from disaster
Is, they say, your daily care:
Can you then deny a plaster
To a wounded virgin here?
Tell me, doughty youth, who cursed thee
With such humors and ill-luck?
Was't some sullen bear dry-nursed thee,
Or she-dragon gave thee suck?
Dulcinea, that virago,
Well may brag of such a Cid,

Now her fame is up, and may go
From Toledo to Madrid.
Would she but her prize surrender,
(Judge how on thy face I dote!)
In exchange I'd gladly send her
My best gown and petticoat.
Happy I, would fortune doom me
But to have me near thy bed,
Stroke thee, pat thee, currycomb thee,
And hunt o'er thy knightly head.
But I ask too much, sincerely,
And I doubt I ne'er must do't,
I'd but kiss your toe, and fairly
Get the length thus of your foot.
How I'd rig thee, and what riches
Should be heaped upon thy bones!
Caps and socks, and cloaks and breeches,
Matchless pearls and precious stones.
Do not from above, like Nero,

See me burn and slight my woe,

But to quench my fires, my hero,

Cast a pitying eye below.

I'm a virgin-pullet, truly;

One more tender ne'er was seen.

A mere chicken fledged but newly;—

Hang me if I'm yet fifteen.

Wind and limb, all's tight about me,

My hair dangles to my feet;

I am straight, too:—if you doubt me,

Trust your eyes, come down and see't.

I've a bob nose has no fellow,

And a sparrow's mouth as rare;

Teeth, like bright topazes, yellow;

Yet I'm deemed a beauty here.

You know what a rare musician

(If you hearken) courts your choice;

I dare say my disposition

Is as taking as my voice.

Here ended the song of the amorous Altisidora, and began the alarm of the courted Don Quixote, who, fetching a deep sigh, said within himself: "Why am I so unhappy a knight-errant that no damsel can see but she must presently fall in love with me? Why is the peerless Dulcinea so unlucky that she must not be suffered singly to enjoy this my incomparable constancy? Queens, what would ye have with her? Empresses, why do ye persecute her? Damsels from fourteen to fifteen, why do ye plague her? Leave, leave the poor creature; let her triumph and glory in the lot which love bestowed upon her in the conquest of my heart and the surrender of my soul. Take notice, enamored multitude, that to Dulcinea alone I am paste and sugar, and to all others flint. To her I am honey, and to the rest of ye aloes. To me, Dulcinea alone is beautiful, discreet, lively, modest, and well-born; all the rest of her sex foul, foolish, fickle, and base-born. To be hers, and hers alone, nature sent me into the world. Let Altisidora weep or sing, let the lady despair on whose account I was buffeted in the castle of the enchanted Moor; boiled or roasted, Dulcinea's I must be, clean, well-bred, and chaste, in spite of all the necromantic powers on earth."

how the great sancho panza took possession of his island, and of the manner of his beginning to govern it.—the governor's wisdom.

O thou ceaseless discoverer of the antipodes, torch of the world, eye of Heaven, and sweet cause of earthen wine coolers; here Thymbrius, there Phœbus; here archer, there physician, father of poesy, inventor of music; thou who always risest, and, though thou seemest to do so, never settest,—to thee I speak, O sun! thee I invoke to favor and enlighten the obscurity of the great Sancho Panza; without thee I find myself indolent, dispirited, and confused!

Sancho, then, with all his attendants, arrived at a town containing about a thousand inhabitants, which was one of the largest and best the duke had. They gave him to understand that it was called the island of Barataria, either because Barataria was really the name of the place, or because he obtained the government of it at so cheap a rate. On his arrival near the gates of the town, which was walled about, the municipal officers came out to receive him. The bells rung, and, with all the demonstrations of a general joy and a great deal of pomp, the people conducted him to the great church to give thanks to God. Presently after, with certain ridiculous ceremonies, they presented him the keys of the town and constituted him perpetual governor of the island of Barataria. The garb, the beard, the thickness and shortness of the new governor, surprised all who were not in the secret, and, indeed, those who were, who were not a few. In fine, as soon as they had brought him out of the church, they carried him to the tribunal of justice and placed him in the chair. The duke's steward then said to him, "It is an ancient custom here, my lord governor, that he who comes to take possession of this famous island is obliged to answer a question put to him, which is to be somewhat intricate and difficult. By his answer the people are enabled to feel the pulse of their new governor's understanding, and, accordingly, are either glad or sorry for his coming."

While the steward was saying this, Sancho was staring at some capital letters written on the wall opposite to his chair, and, being unable to read, he asked what that writing was on the wall. He was answered, "Sir, it is there written on what day your honor took possession of this island. The inscription runs thus: 'This day, such a day of the month and year, Signor Don Sancho Panza took possession of this island. Long may he enjoy it.'"

"Pray who is it they call Don Sancho Panza?" demanded Sancho.

"Your lordship," answered the steward! "for no other Panza, besides him now in the chair, ever came into this island."

"Take notice, then, brother," returned Sancho, "that the Don does not belong to me, nor ever did to any of my family. I am called plain Sancho Panza: my father was a Sancho, and my grandfather was a Sancho, and they were all Panzas, without any addition of Dons, or any other title whatever. I fancy there are more Dons than stones in this island. But enough: God knows my meaning: and perhaps, if my government lasts four days, I may weed out these Dons that over-run the country, and, by their numbers, are as troublesome as mosquitoes and cousins. On with your question, Master Steward, and I will answer the best I can, let the people be sorry or rejoice."

About this time two men came into the court, the one clad like a country fellow, and the other like a tailor, with a pair of shears in his hand; and the tailor said: "My lord governor, I and this countryman come before your worship by reason this honest man came yesterday to my shop (saving your presence, I am a tailor, and have passed my examination, God be thanked), and putting a piece of cloth into my hands, asked me, 'Sir, is there enough of this to make me a cap?' I, measuring the piece, answered Yes. Now he bade me view it again, and see if there was not enough for two. I guessed his drift, and told him there was. Persisting in his knavish intentions, my customer went on increasing the number of caps, and I still saying yes, till we came to five caps. A little time ago he came to claim them. I offered them to him, but he refuses to pay me for the making, and insists I shall either return him his cloth, or pay him for it."

"Is all this so, brother?" demanded Sancho.

"Yes," answered the man; "but pray, my lord, make him produce the five caps he has made me."

"With all my heart," answered the tailor; and pulling his hand from under his cloak, he showed the five caps on the ends of his fingers and thumb, saying: "Here are the five caps this honest man would have me make, and on my soul and conscience, not a shred of the cloth is left, and I submit the work to be viewed by any inspectors of the trade."

All present laughed at the number of the caps and the novelty of the suit. Sancho reflected a moment, and then said: "I am of opinion there needs no great delay in this suit, and it may be decided very equitably off-hand. Therefore I pronounce, that the tailor lose the making, and the countryman the stuff, and that the caps be confiscated to the use of the poor: and there is an end of that."

If the sentence Sancho afterwards passed on the purse of the herdsman caused the admiration of all the bystanders, this excited their laughter. However, what the governor commanded was executed, and two old men next presented themselves before him. One of them carried a cane in his hand for a staff; the other, who had no staff, said to Sancho: "My lord, some time ago I lent this man ten crowns of gold to oblige and serve him, upon condition that he should return them on demand. I let some time pass without asking for them, being loth to put him to a greater strait to pay me than he was in when I lent them. But at length, thinking it full time to be repaid, I asked him for my money more than once, but to no purpose: he not only refuses payment, but denies the debt, and says I never lent him any such sum, or, if I did that he had already paid me. I have no witnesses to the loan, nor has he of the payment which he pretends to have made, but which I deny; yet if he will swear before your worship that he has returned the money, I from this minute acquit him before God and the world."

"What say you to this, old gentleman?" quoth Sancho.

"I confess, my lord," replied the old fellow, "that he did lend me the money, and if your worship pleases to hold down your wand of justice, since he leaves it to my oath, I will swear I have really and truly returned it to him."

The governor accordingly held down his wand, and the old fellow, seeming encumbered with his staff, gave it to his creditor to hold while he was swearing; and then taking hold of the cross of the wand, he said it was true indeed the other had lent him ten crowns, but that he had restored them to him into his own hand; but having, he supposed, forgotten it, he was continually dunning him for them. Upon which his lordship the governor demanded of the creditor what he had to say in reply to the solemn declaration he had heard. He said that he submitted, and could not doubt but that his debtor had sworn the truth; for he believed him to be an honest man and a good Christian; and that, as the fault must have been in his own memory, he would thenceforward ask him no more for his money. The debtor now took his staff again, and bowing to the governor, went out of court.

Sancho having observed the defendant take his staff and walk away, and noticing also the resignation of the plaintiff, he began to meditate, and laying the fore-finger of his right hand upon his forehead, he continued a short time apparently full of thought; and then raising his head, he ordered the old man with the staff to be called back; and when he had returned, "Honest friend," said the governor, "give me that staff, for I have occasion for it."

"With all my heart," answered the old fellow; and delivered it into his hand. Sancho took it, and giving it to the other old man, said: "Go about your business, in God's name, for you are paid." "I, my lord," answered the old man; "what! is this cane worth ten golden crowns?"

"Yes," quoth the governor, "or I am the greatest dunce in the world! and now it shall appear whether I have a head to govern a whole kingdom." Straight he commanded the cane to be broken before them all. Which being done there were found in the hollow of it ten crowns in gold.

All were struck with admiration, and took their new governor for a second Solomon. They asked him, whence he had collected that the ten crowns were in the cane. He answered, that upon seeing the old man give it his adversary, while he was taking the oath, and swearing that he had really and truly restored them into his own hands, and, when he had done, ask for it again, it came into his imagination, the money in dispute must be in the hollow of the cane. Whence it may be gathered, that, God Almighty often directs the judgment of those who govern, though otherwise mere blockheads: besides, he had heard the priest of his parish tell a like case; and, were it not that he was so unlucky as to forget all he had a mind to remember, his memory was so good, there would not have been a better in the whole island.

At length, both the old men marched off, the one ashamed, and the other satisfied; the bystanders were surprised, and the secretary, who minuted down the words, actions, and behavior of Sancho Panza, could not determine with himself, whether he should set him down for a wise man or a fool. All the court were in admiration at the acuteness and wisdom of their new governor; all of whose sentences and decrees, being noted down by the appointed historiographer, were immediately transmitted to the duke, who waited for these accounts with the utmost impatience.

We see that governors, though otherwise fools, are sometimes directed in their decisions by the hand of God.

Time is ever moving; nothing ever can impede his course.

An understanding in the beginning is often an effectual cure for those who are indiscreetly in love.

At eleven o'clock Don Quixote retired to his apartment, and finding a lute there, he tuned it, opened the window, and, perceiving there was somebody walking in the garden, he ran over the strings of the instrument; and, having tuned it again as nicely as he could, he coughed and cleared his throat; and then, with a voice somewhat hoarse, yet not unmusical, he sang the following song, which he had composed himself that very day:—

THE ADVICE.

matteaux's translation.

Love, a strong, designing foe.

Careless hearts with ease deceives;

Can thy breast resist his blow,

Which your sloth unguarded leaves?

If you're idle you're destroyed,
All his art on you he tries;
But be watchful and employed,
Straight the baffled tempter flies.
Maids for modest grace admired,
If they would their fortunes raise,
Must in silence live retired:
'Tis their virtue speaks their praise.
The divine Tobosan fair,
Dulcinea, claims me whole;
Nothing can her image tear!
'Tis one substance with my soul.

Then let fortune smile or frown,
Nothing shall my faith remove;
Constant truth, the lover's crown,
Can work miracles in love.
the same as translated by smollett.
Love, with idleness combined,
Will unhinge the tender mind:
But to few, to work and move,
Will exclude the force of love.
Blooming maids that would be married,
Must in virtue be unwearied;
Modesty a dower will raise,
And be a trumpet of their praise.
A cavalier will sport and play
With a damsel frank and gay;
But, when wedlock is his aim,
Choose a maid of sober fame.

Passion kindled in the breast,
By a stranger or a guest,
Enters with the rising sun,
And fleets before his race be run:
Love that comes so suddenly,
Ever on the wing to fly,
Neither can nor will impart
Strong impressions to the heart.
Pictures drawn on pictures, show
Strange confusion to the view:
Second beauty finds no base,
Where a first has taken place:
Then Dulcinea still shall reign

Without a rival or a stain;
Nor shall fate itself control
Her sway, or blot her from my soul:
Constancy, the lover's boast,
I'll maintain whate'er it cost:
This, my virtue will refine;
This will stamp my joys divine.
the same as translated by jarvis.
Love, with idleness is friend,
O'er a maiden gains its end:
But let business and employment
Fill up every careful moment;
These an antidote will prove
'Gainst the pois'nous arts of love.
Maidens that aspire to marry,
In their looks reserve should carry:

Modesty their price should raise,
And be the herald of their praise.
Knights, whom toils of arms employ,
With the free may laugh and toy;
But the modest only, choose
When they tie the nuptial noose.
Love that rises with the sun,
With his setting beams is gone:
Love that guest-like visits hearts,
When the banquet's o'er, departs:
And the love that comes to-day,
And to-morrow wings its way,
Leaves no traces on the soul,
Its affections to control.

Where a sovereign beauty reigns,
Fruitless are a rival's pains,—
O'er a finished picture who
E'er a second picture drew?
Fair Dulcinea, queen of beauty,
Rules my heart, and claims its duty,
Nothing there can take her place,
Naught her image can erase.
Whether fortune smile or frown,
Constancy 's the lover's crown;
And, its force divine to prove,
Miracles performs in love.

THE GOVERNOR IN A RAGE

The history relates that Sancho Panza was conducted from the court of justice to a sumptuous palace, where in a great hall he found a magnificent entertainment prepared. He had no sooner entered than his ears were saluted by the sound of many instruments, and four pages served him with water to wash his hands, which the governor received with becoming gravity. The music having ceased, Sancho now sat down to dinner in a chair of state placed at the upper end of the table, for there was but one seat and only one plate and napkin. A personage, who, as it afterwards appeared, was a physician, took his stand at one side of his chair with a whalebone rod in his hand. They then removed the beautiful white cloth, which covered a variety of fruits and other eatables. Grace was said by one in a student's dress, and a laced bib was placed by a page under Sancho's chin. Another, who performed the office of sewer, now set a plate of fruit before him; but he had scarcely tasted it, when, on being touched by the wand-bearer, it was snatched away, and another containing meat instantly supplied its place. Yet before Sancho could make a beginning it vanished, like the former, on a signal of the wand.

The governor was surprised at this proceeding, and looking around him, asked if this dinner was only to show off their sleight of hand.

"My lord," said the wand-bearer, "your lordship's food must here be watched with the same care as is customary with the governors of other islands. I am a doctor of physic, sir, and my duty, for which I receive a salary, is to watch over the governor's health, whereof I am more careful than of my own. I study his constitution night and day, that I may know how to restore him when sick; and therefore think it incumbent on me to pay especial regard to his meals, at which I constantly preside, to see that he eats what is good and salutary, and prevent his touching whatever I imagine may be prejudicial to his health or offensive to his stomach. It was for that reason, my lord," continued he, "I ordered the dish of fruit to be taken away, as being too watery, and that other dish, as being too hot and over-seasoned with spices, which are apt to provoke thirst; and he that drinks much destroys and consumes the radical moisture, which is the fuel of life."

"Well, then," quoth Sancho, "that plate of roasted partridges, which seem to me to be very well seasoned, I suppose will do me no manner of harm?"

"Hold," said the doctor, "my lord governor shall not eat them while I live to prevent it."

"Pray, why not?" quoth Sancho.

"Because," answered the doctor, "our great master Hippocrates, the north star and luminary of medicine, says in one of his aphorisms, Omnis saturatio mala, perdicis autem pessima; which means, 'All repletion is bad, but that from partridges the worst.'"

"If it be so," quoth Sancho, "pray cast your eye, signor doctor, over all these dishes here on the table, and see which will do me the most good or the least harm, and let me eat of it without whisking it away with your conjuring-stick; for, by my soul, and as Heaven shall give me life to enjoy this government, I am dying with hunger; and to deny me food—let signor doctor say what he will—is not the way to lengthen my life, but to cut it short."

"Your worship is in the right, my lord governor," answered the physician, "and therefore I am of opinion you should not eat of these stewed rabbits, as being a food that is tough and acute; of that veal, indeed, you might have taken a little, had it been neither roasted nor stewed; but as it is, not a morsel."

"What think you, then," said Sancho, "of that huge dish there, smoking hot, which I take to be an olla-podrida?—for, among the many things contained in it, I surely may light upon something both wholesome and toothsome."

"Absit!" quoth the doctor, "far be such a thought from us. Olla-podrida! there is no worse dish in the world. Leave them to prebends and rectors of colleges or lusty feeders at country weddings; but let them not be seen on the tables of governors, where nothing contrary to health and delicacy should be tolerated. Simple medicines are always more estimable and safe, for in them there can be no mistake, whereas in such as are compounded all is hazard and uncertainty. Therefore, what I would at present advise my lord governor to eat, in order to corroborate and preserve his health, is about a hundred small rolled-up wafers, with some thin slices of marmalade, that may sit upon the stomach and help digestion."

Sancho, hearing this, threw himself backward in his chair, and looking at the doctor from head to foot very seriously, asked him his name and where he had studied. To which he answered, "My lord governor, my name is Doctor Pedro Rezio de Aguero; I am a native of a place called Tirteafuera, lying between Caraquel and Almoddobar del Campo, on the right hand, and I have taken my doctor's degrees in the university of Ossuna."

"Then, hark you," said Sancho in a rage, "Signor Doctor Pedro Rezzio de Aguero, native of Tirteafuera, lying on the right hand as we go from Caraquel to Almoddobar del Campo, graduate in Ossuna, get out of my sight this instant, or, by the light of Heaven, I will take a cudgel, and, beginning with your carcass, will so belabor all the physic-mongers in the island, that not one of the tribe shall be left!—I mean of those like yourself, who are ignorant quacks. For those who are learned and wise I shall make much of and honor as so many angels. I say again, Signor Pedro Rezio, begone, or I shall take the chair I sit on and comb your head to some tune; and if I am called to an account for it when I give up my office, I shall prove that I have done a good service in ridding the world of a bad physician, who is a public executioner. Body of me! give me something to eat, or let them take back their government,—for an office that will not find a man in victuals is not worth two beans."

On seeing the governor in such a fury the doctor would have fled out in the hall had not the sound of a courier's horn at that instant been heard in the street. "A courier from my lord duke," said the sewer (who had looked out of the window), "and he must certainly have brought despatches of importance."

The courier entered hastily, foaming with sweat and in great agitation, and pulling a packet out of his bosom, he delivered it into the governor's hands, and by him it was given to the steward, telling him to read the superscription, which was this: "To Don Sancho Panza, Governor of the Island of Barataria. To be delivered only to himself or to his secretary."

"Who is my secretary?" said Sancho.

"It is I, my lord," answered one who was present, "for I can read and write, and am, besides, a Biscayan."

"With that addition," quoth Sancho, "you may very well be secretary to the emperor himself. Open the packet and see what it holds."

The new secretary did so, and having run his eye over the contents, he said it was a business which required privacy. Accordingly, Sancho commanded all to retire excepting the steward and sewer; and when the hall was cleared, the secretary read the following letter:—

"It has just come to my knowledge, Signor Don Panza, that certain enemies of mine intend very soon to make a desperate attack, by night, upon the island under your command; it is necessary, therefore, to be vigilant and alert, that you may not be taken by surprise. I have also received intelligence from trusty spies, that four persons in disguise are now in your town, sent thither by the enemy, who, fearful of your great talents, have a design upon your life. Keep a strict watch, be careful who are admitted to you, and eat nothing sent you as a present. I will not fail to send you assistance if you are in want of it. Whatever may be attempted, I have full reliance on your activity and judgment.

"Your friend,

"The Duke.

"From this place, the th of August,

    at four in the morning."

Sancho was astonished at this information, and the others appeared to be no less so. At length, turning to the steward, "I will tell you," said he, "the first thing to be done, which is to clap Doctor Rezio into a dungeon; for if anybody has a design to kill me, it is he, and that by the most lingering and the worst of all deaths,—starvation."

"Be that as it may," said the steward, "it is my opinion your honor would do well to eat none of the meat here upon the table, for it was presented by some nuns, and it is a saying, 'The devil lurks behind the cross.'"

"You are in the right," quoth Sancho, "and for the present give me only a piece of bread and some four pounds of grapes,—there can be no poison in them,—for, in truth, I cannot live without food, and if we must keep in readiness for these battles that threaten us, it is fit that we should be well fed, for the stomach upholds the heart and the heart the man. Do you, Mr. Secretary, answer the letter of my lord duke, and tell him his commands shall be obeyed throughout most faithfully; and present my dutiful respects to my lady duchess, and beg her not to forget to send a special messenger with my letter and bundle to my wife Teresa Panza, which I shall take as a particular favor, and will be her humble servant to the utmost of my power. And, by the way, you may put in my hearty service to my master, Don Quixote de la Mancha, that he may see that I am neither forgetful nor ungrateful; and as to the rest, I leave it to you, as a good secretary and a true Biscayan, to add whatever you please, or that may turn to the best account. Now away with this cloth, and bring me something that may be eaten, and then let these spies, murderers, and enchanters see how they meddle with me or my island."

A page now entered, saying, "Here is a countryman who would speak with your lordship on business, as he says, of great importance."

"It is very strange," quoth Sancho, "that these men of business should be so silly as not to see that this is not a time for such matters. What! we who govern and belike are not made of flesh and bone like other men! We are made of marble-stone, forsooth, and have no need of rest or refreshment! Before Heaven and upon my conscience, if my government lasts, as I have a glimmering it will not, I shall hamper more than one of these men of business! Well, for this once, tell the fellow to come in; but first see that he is no spy, nor one of my murderers."

"He looks, my lord," answered the page, "like a simple fellow, and I am much mistaken if he be not as harmless as a crust of bread."

"Your worship need not fear," quoth the steward, "since we are with you."

"But now that Doctor Pedro Rezio is gone," quoth Sancho, "may I not have something to eat of substance and weight, though it were but a luncheon of bread and an onion?"

"At night your honor shall have no cause to complain," quoth the sewer; "supper shall make up for the want of dinner."

"Heaven grant it may," replied Sancho.

THE COUNTRYMAN'S TALE

The countryman, who was of goodly presence, then came in, and it might be seen a thousand leagues off that he was an honest, good soul.

"Which among you here is the lord governor?" said he.

"Who should it be," answered the secretary, "but he who is seated in the chair?"

"I humble myself in his presence," quoth the countryman; and kneeling down, he begged for his hand to kiss.

Sancho refused it, and commanded him to rise and tell his business. The countryman did so, and said: "My lord, I am a husbandman, a native of Miguel Terra, two leagues from Ciudad Real."

"What! another Tirteafuera?" quoth Sancho. "Say on, brother; for let me tell you, I know Miguel Terra very well; it is not very far from my own village."

"The business is this, sir," continued the peasant: "by the mercy of Heaven I was married in peace and in the face of the holy Roman Catholic Church. I have two sons, bred scholars; the younger studies for bachelor, and the elder for licentiate. I am a widower, for my wife died, or rather a wicked physician killed her by improper medicines when she was pregnant; and if it had been God's will that the child had been born, and had proved a son, I would have put him to study for doctor, that he might not envy his two brothers, the bachelor and the licentiate."

"So that, if your wife," quoth Sancho, "had not died, or had not been killed, you would not now be a widower."

"No, certainly, my lord," answered the peasant.

"We are much the nearer," replied Sancho; "go on, friend, for this is an hour rather for bed than business."

"I say, then," quoth the countryman, "that my son who is to be the bachelor fell in love with a damsel in the same village, called Clara Perlerino, daughter of Andres Perlerino, a very rich farmer; which name of Perlerino came to them not by lineal or any other descent, but because all of that race are paralytic; and to mend the name, they call them Perlerinos. Indeed, to say the truth, the damsel is like any oriental pearl, and looked at on the right side seems a very flower of the field; but on the left not quite so fair, for on that side she wants an eye, which she lost by the small-pox; and though the pits in her face are many and deep, her admirers say they are not pits but graves wherein the hearts of her lovers are buried. So clean and delicate, too, is she, that to prevent defiling her face, she carries her nose so hooked up that it seems to fly from her mouth; yet for all that she looks charmingly, for she has a large mouth, and did she not lack half a score or a dozen front teeth she might pass and make a figure among the fairest. I say nothing of her lips, for they are so thin that, were it the fashion to reel lips, one might make a skein of them; but, being of a different color from what is usual in lips, they have a marvellous appearance, for they are streaked with blue, green, and orange-tawny. Pardon me, good my lord governor, if I paint so minutely the parts of her who is about to become my daughter; for in truth I love and admire her more than I can tell."

"Paint what you will," quoth Sancho, "for I am mightily taken with the picture; and had I but dined, I would not desire a better dessert than your portrait."

"It shall be always at your service," answered the peasant; "and the time may come when we may be acquainted, though we are not so now; and I assure you, my lord, if I could but paint her genteelness and the tallness of her person, you would admire: but that cannot be, because she is crooked, and crumpled up together, and her knees touch her mouth; though, for all that, you may see plainly that could she but stand upright she would touch the ceiling with her head. And she would ere now have given her hand to my bachelor to be his wife, but that she cannot stretch it out, it is so shrunk; nevertheless, her long guttered nails show the goodness of its make."

"So far so good," quoth Sancho; "and now, brother, make account that you have painted her from head to foot. What is it you would be at? Come to the point without so many windings and turnings, so many fetches and digressions."

"What I desire, my lord," answered the countryman, "is, that your lordship would do me the favor to give me a letter of recommendation to her father, begging his consent to the match, since we are pretty equal in our fortunes and natural endowments; for, to say the truth, my lord governor, my son is possessed, and scarcely a day passes in which the evil spirits do not torment him three or four times; and having thereby once fallen into the fire, his face is as shrivelled as a piece of scorched parchment, and his eyes are somewhat bleared and running; but, bless him! he has the temper of an angel, and did he not buffet and belabor himself, he would be a very saint for gentleness."

"Would you have anything else, honest friend?" said Sancho.

"One thing more I would ask," quoth the peasant, "but I dare not,—yet out it shall; come what may, it shall not rot in my breast. I say then, my lord, I could wish your worship to give me three or six hundred ducats towards mending the fortunes of my bachelor,—I mean, to assist in furnishing his house; for it is agreed that they shall live by themselves, without being subject to the impertinences of their fathers-in-law."

"Well," quoth Sancho, "see if there is anything else you would have, and be not squeamish in asking."

"No, nothing more," answered the peasant.

The governor then rising, and seizing the chair on which he had been seated, exclaimed, "I vow to Heaven, Don Lubberly, saucy bumpkin, if you do not instantly get out of my sight, I will break your head with this chair! Son of a rascal, and the devil's own painter! At this time of day to come and ask me for six hundred ducats! Where should I have them, villain? And if I had them, idiot! why should I give them to thee? What care I for Miguel Terra, or for the whole race of the Perlerinos? Begone, I say! or, by the life of my lord duke, I will be as good as my word. Thou art no native of Miguel Terra, but some scoffer sent from the devil to tempt me. Impudent scoundrel! I have not yet had the government a day and a half, and you expect I should have six hundred ducats!"

The sewer made signs to the countryman to go out of the hall, which he did, hanging down his head, and seemingly much afraid lest the governor should put his threat into execution,—for the knave knew very well how to play his part.

But let us leave Sancho in his passion; peace be with him!

The devil will never give you a high nose if a flat nose will serve your turn.

All is not gold that glitters.

I am fully convinced that judges and governors are, or ought to be, made of brass, so as that they may not feel the importunity of people of business, who expect to be heard and despatched at all hours and at all seasons, come what will, attending only to their own affairs; and if the poor devil of a judge does not hear and despatch them, either because it is not in his power, or it happens to be an unseasonable time for giving audience, then they grumble and backbite, gnaw him to the very bones, and even bespatter his whole generation. Ignorant man of business! foolish man of business! be not in such a violent hurry; wait for the proper season and conjuncture, and come not at meals and sleeping-time; for judges are made of flesh and blood, and must give to nature that which nature requires.

Good physicians deserve palms and laurels.

Either we are, or we are not.

Walls have ears.

Let us all live and eat together in harmony and good friendship.

When God sends the morning, the light shines upon all.

Make yourselves honey, and the flies will devour you.

Your idle and lazy people in a commonwealth are like drones in a beehive, which only devour the honey the laboring bees gather.

Every day produces something new in the world: jests turn into earnest, and the biters are bit.

They who expect snacks should be modest, and take cheerfully whatever is given them, and not haggle with the winners; unless they know them to be sharpers, and their gains unfairly gotten.

THE GOVERNOR'S ROUND OF INSPECTION

After traversing a few streets, they heard the clashing of swords, and, hastening to the place, they found two men fighting. On seeing the officers coming they desisted, and one of them said, "Help, in the name of Heaven and the king! Are people to be attacked here, and robbed in the open streets?"

"Hold, honest man," quoth Sancho, "and tell me what is the occasion of this fray; for I am the governor."

His antagonist, interposing, said, "My lord governor, ernor, I will briefly relate the matter:—Your honor must know that this gentleman is just come from the gaming-house over the way, where he has been winning above a thousand reals, and heaven knows how, except that I, happening to be present, was induced, even against my conscience, to give judgment in his favor in many a doubtful point; and when I expected he would have given me something, though it were but the small matter of a crown, by way of present, as it is usual with gentlemen of character like myself, who stand by, ready to back unreasonable demands, and to prevent quarrels, up he got, with his pockets filled, and marched out of the house.

"Surprised and vexed at such conduct, I followed him, civilly reminded him that he could not refuse me the small sum of eight reals, as he knew me to be a man of honor, without either office or pension; my parents having brought me up to nothing: yet this knave, who is as great a thief as Cacus, and as arrant a sharper as Andradilla, would give me but four reals! Think, my lord governor, what a shameless and unconscionable fellow he is! But as I live had it not been for your worship coming, I would have made him disgorge his winnings, and taught him how to balance accounts."

"What shall be done," replied Sancho, "is this: you, master winner, whether by fair play or foul, instantly give your hackster here a hundred reals, and pay down thirty more for the poor prisoners; and you, sir, who have neither office nor pension, nor honest employment, take the hundred reals, and, some time to-morrow, be sure you get out of this island, nor set foot in it again these ten years, unless you would finish your banishment in the next life: for if I find you here, I will make you swing on a gibbet—at least the hangman shall do it for me: so let no man reply, or he shall repent it."

The decree was immediately executed: the one disbursed, the other received; the one quitted the island, the other went home.

Cheats are always at the mercy of their accomplices.

The maid that would keep her good name, stays at home as if she were lame. A hen and a housewife, whatever they cost, if once they go gadding will surely be lost. And she that longs to see, I ween, is as desirous to be seen.

Good fortune wants only a beginning.

When they offer thee a government, lay hold of it.

When an earldom is put before thee, lay thy clutches on it.

When they throw thee some beneficial bone, snap at the favor; if not, sleep on and never answer to good fortune and preferment when they knock at thy door.

Truth will always rise uppermost, as oil rises above water.

Seeing is believing.

According to reason, each thing has its season.

When justice is doubtful, I should lean to the side of mercy.

A MESSENGER TO TERESA PANZA

Being desirous to please his lord and lady, he set off with much glee to Sancho's village. Having arrived near it, he inquired of some women whom he saw washing in a brook if there lived not in that town one Teresa Panza, wife of one Sancho Panza, squire to a knight called Don Quixote de la Mancha.

"That Teresa Panza is my mother," said a young lass who was washing among the rest, "and that Sancho my own father, and that knight our master."

"Are they so?" quoth the page: "come then, my good girl, and lead me to your mother, for I have a letter and a token for her from that same father of yours."

"That I will, with all my heart, sir," answered the girl (who seemed to be about fourteen years of age); and leaving the linen she was washing to one of her companions, without stopping to cover either her head or feet, away she ran skipping along before the page's horse, bare-legged, and her hair dishevelled.

"Come along, sir, an 't please you," quoth she, "for our house stands hard by, and you will find my mother in trouble enough for being so long without tidings of my father."

"Well," said the page, "I now bring her news that will cheer her heart, I warrant her."

So on he went, with his guide running, skipping, and capering before him, till they reached the village, and, before she got up to the house, she called out aloud, "Mother, mother, come out! here's a gentleman who brings letters and other things from my good father."

At these words out came her mother Teresa Panza with a distaff in her hand—for she was spinning flax. She was clad in a russet petticoat, so short that it looked as if it had been docked at the placket, with a jacket of the same, and the sleeves of her under-garment hanging about it. She appeared to be about forty years of age and was strong, hale, sinewy, and hard as a hazel-nut.

"What is the matter, girl?" quoth she, seeing her daughter with the page; "what gentleman is that?"

"It is an humble servant of my Lady Donna Teresa Panza," answered the page; and throwing himself from his horse, with great respect he went and kneeled before the Lady Teresa, saying, "Be pleased, Signora Donna Teresa, to give me your ladyship's hand to kiss, as the lawful wife of Signor Don Sancho Panza, sole governor of the island of Barataria."

"Alack-a-day, good sir, how you talk!" she replied: "I am no court-dame, but a poor country woman, daughter of a ploughman, and wife indeed of a squire-errant, but no governor."

"Your ladyship," answered the page, "is the most worthy wife of a thrice-worthy governor, and to confirm the truth of what I say, be pleased, madam, to receive what I here bring you."

He then drew the letter from his pocket, and a string of corals, each bead set in gold, and, putting it about her neck, he said, "This letter is from my lord governor, and another that I have here, and those corals are from my lady duchess, who sends me to your ladyship."

Teresa and her daughter were all astonishment.

"May I die," said the girl, "if our master Don Quixote be not at the bottom of this—as sure as day he has given my father the government or earldom he has so often promised him."

"It is even so," answered the page; "and for Signor Don Quixote's sake, my Lord Sancho is now governor of the island of Barataria, as the letter will inform you."

"Pray, young gentleman," quoth Teresa, "be pleased to read it; for though I can spin I cannot read a jot."

"Nor I neither, i' faith," cried Sanchica; "but stay a little, and I will fetch one who can, either the bachelor Sampson Carrasco or the priest himself, who will come with all their hearts to hear news of my father."

"You need not take that trouble," said the page; "for I can read though I cannot spin, and will read it to you." Which he accordingly did: but as its contents have already been given, it is not here repeated. He then produced the letter from the duchess, and read as follows:—

"Friend Teresa,—

"Finding your husband Sancho worthy of my esteem for his honesty and good understanding, I prevailed upon the duke, my spouse, to make him governor of one of the many islands in his possession. I am informed he governs like any hawk; at which I and my lord duke are mightily pleased, and give many thanks to Heaven that I have not been deceived in my choice, for madam Teresa may be assured that it is no easy matter to find a good governor —and God make me as good as Sancho governs well. I have sent you, my dear friend, a string of corals set in gold—I wish they were oriental pearls; but whoever gives thee a bone has no mind to see thee dead: the time will come when we shall be better acquainted, and converse with each other, and then heaven knows what may happen. Commend me to your daughter Sanchica, and tell her from me to get herself ready; for I mean to have her highly married when she least expects it. I am told the acorns near your town are very large—pray send me some two dozen of them; for I shall value them the more as coming from your hand. Write to me immediately, to inform me of your health and welfare; and if you want anything, you need but open your mouth, and it shall be measured. So God keep you.

"Your loving Friend,

"The Duchess.

"From this place."

"Ah!" quoth Teresa, at hearing the letter, "how good, how plain, how humble a lady! let me be buried with such ladies as this, say I and not with such proud madams as this town affords, who think because they are gentlefolks, the wind must not blow upon them; and go flaunting to church as if they were queens! they seem to think it a disgrace to look upon a peasant woman: and yet you see how this good lady, though she be a duchess, calls me friend, and treats me as if I were her equal!—and equal may I see her to the highest steeple in La Mancha! As to the acorns, sir, I will send her ladyship a peck of them, and such as, for their size, people shall come from far and near to see and admire. But for the present, Sanchica, let us make much of this gentleman. Do thou take care of his horse, child, and bring some new-laid eggs out of the stable, and slice some rashers of bacon, and let us entertain him like any prince; for his good news and his own good looks deserve no less."

Sanchica now came in with her lap full of eggs. "Pray, sir," said she to the page, "does my father, now he is a governor, wear trunk-hose?"

"I never observed," answered the page, "but doubtless he does."

"God's my life!" replied Sanchica, "what a sight to see my father in long breeches? Is it not strange that ever since I was born I have longed to see my father with breeches of that fashion laced to his girdle?"

"I warrant you will have that pleasure if you live," answered the page; "before Heaven, if his government lasts but two months, he is likely to travel with a cape to his cap."

OF THE PROGRESS OF SANCHO PANZA'S GOVERNMENT

The first business that occurred on that day was an appeal to his judgment in a case which was thus stated by a stranger—the appellant: "My lord," said he, "there is a river which passes through the domains of a certain lord, dividing it into two parts—I beseech your honor to give me your attention, for it is a case of great importance and some difficulty. I say, then, that upon this river there was a bridge, and at one end of it a gallows and a kind of courthouse, where four judges sit to try, and pass sentence upon those who are found to transgress a certain law enacted by the proprietor, which runs thus: 'Whoever would pass over this bridge must first declare upon oath whence he comes, and upon what business he is going; and if he swears the truth, he shall pass over; but if he swears to a falsehood, he shall certainly die upon a gibbet there provided.'

"After this law was made known, many persons ventured over it, and the truth of what they swore being admitted, they were allowed freely to pass. But a man now comes demanding a passage over the bridge; and, on taking the required oath, he swears that he is going to be executed upon the gibbet before him, and that he has no other business. The judges deliberated, but would not decide. 'If we let this man pass freely,' said they, 'he will have sworn falsely, and by the law, he ought to die: and, if we hang him, he will verify his oath, and he, having sworn the truth, ought to have passed unmolested as the law ordains.' The case, my lord, is yet suspended, for the judges know not how to act; and, therefore having heard of your lordship's great wisdom and acuteness, they have sent me humbly to beseech your lordship on their behalf, to give your opinion in so intricate and perplexing a case."

"To deal plainly with you," said Sancho, "these gentlemen judges who sent you to me might have saved themselves and you the labor; for I have more of the blunt than the acute in me. However, let me hear your question once more, that I may understand it the better, and mayhap I may chance to hit the right nail on the head."

The man accordingly told his tale once or twice more, and when he had done, the governor thus delivered his opinion: "To my thinking," said he, "this matter may soon be settled; and I will tell you how. The man, you say, swears he is going to die upon the gallows; and if he is hanged, it would be against the law, because he swore the truth; and if they do not hang him, why then he swore a lie, and ought to have suffered."

"It is just as you say, my lord governor," said the messenger, "and nothing more is wanting to a right understanding of the case."

"I say, then," continued Sancho, "that they must let that part of the man pass that swore the truth and hang that part that swore the lie, and thereby the law will be obeyed."

"If so, my lord," replied the stranger, "the man must be divided into two parts; and thereby he will certainly die, and thus the law, which we are bound to observe, is in no respect complied with."

"Harkee, honest man," said Sancho, "either I have no brains, or there is as much reason to put this passenger to death as to let him live and pass the bridge; for, if the truth saves him, the lie also condemns him, and this being so, you may tell those gentlemen who sent you to me, that since the reasons for condemning and acquitting him are equal, they should let the man pass freely, for it is always more commendable to do good than to do harm."

Sancho having plentifully dined that day, in spite of all the aphorisms of Dr. Tirteafuera, when the cloth was removed in came an express with a letter from Don Quixote to the governor. Sancho ordered the secretary to read it to himself, and if there was nothing in it for secret perusal, then to read it aloud. The secretary having first run it over, accordingly, "My lord," said he, "the letter may not only be publicly read, but deserves to be engraved in characters of gold; and thus it is:—"

DON QUIXOTE DE LA MANCHA TO SANCHO PANZA, GOVERNOR OF THE ISLAND OF BARATARIA.

"When I expected to have had an account of thy carelessness and blunders, friend Sancho, I was agreeably disappointed with news of thy wise behavior, —for which I return thanks to Heaven, that can raise the lowest from their poverty and turn the fool into a man of sense. I hear thou governest with all discretion; and that, nevertheless, thou retainest the humility of the meanest creature. But I would observe to thee, Sancho, that it is often expedient and necessary, for the due support of authority, to act in contradiction to the humility of the heart. The personal adornments of one that is raised to a high situation must correspond with his present greatness, and not with his former lowliness. Let thy apparel, therefore, be good and becoming; for the hedgestake, when decorated no longer, appears what it really is. I do not mean that thou shouldst wear jewels or finery; nor, being a judge, would I have thee dress like a soldier; but adorn thyself in a manner suitable to thy employment. To gain the good-will of thy people, two things, among others, thou must not fail to observe: one is, to be courteous to all,—that, indeed, I have already told thee; the other is, to take especial care that the people be exposed to no scarcity of food, for, with the poor, hunger is, of all afflictions, the most insupportable. Publish few edicts, but let those be good; and, above all, see that they are well observed, for edicts that are not kept are the same as not made, and serve only to show that the prince, though he had wisdom and authority to make them had not the courage to insist upon their execution. Laws that threaten and are not enforced become like King Log, whose croaking subjects first feared, then despised him. Be a father to virtue and a step-father to vice. Be not always severe, nor always mild; but choose the happy mean between them, which is the true point of discretion. Visit the prisons, the shambles, and the markets; for there the presence of the governor is highly necessary. Such attention is a comfort to the prisoner hoping for release; it is a terror to the butchers, who then dare not make use of false weights; and the same effect is produced on all other dealers. Shouldst thou unhappily be secretly inclined to avarice, to gluttony, or women,—which I hope thou art not,—avoid showing thyself guilty of these vices; for, when those who are concerned with thee discover thy ruling passion, they will assault thee on that quarter, nor leave thee till they have effected thy destruction. View and review, consider and reconsider, the counsels and documents I gave thee in writing before thy departure hence to thy government, and in them thou wilt find a choice supply to sustain thee through the toils and difficulties which governors must continually encounter. Write to thy patrons, the duke and duchess, and show thyself grateful, for ingratitude is the daughter of pride, and one of the greatest sins; whereas, he who is grateful to those that have done him service, thereby testifies that he will be grateful also to God, his constant benefactor.

"My lady duchess has despatched a messenger to thy wife Teresa with thy hunting-suit, and also a present from herself. We expect an answer every moment. I have been a little out of order with a certain cat-clawing which befell me, not much to the advantage of my nose; but it was nothing, for if there are enchanters who persecute me, there are others who defend me. Let me know if the steward who is with thee had any hand in the actions of the Trifaldi, as thou hast suspected; and give me advice, from time to time, of all that happens to thee, since the distance between us is so short. I think of quitting this idle life very soon, for I was not born for luxury and ease. A circumstance has occurred which may, I believe, tend to deprive me of the favor of the duke and duchess; but, though it afflicts me much, it affects not my determination, for I must comply with the duties of my profession in preference to any other claim; as it is often said, Amicus Plato, sed magis amica veritas. I write this in Latin, being persuaded that thou hast learned that language since thy promotion. Farewell, and God have thee in His keeping; so mayst thou escape the pity of the world.

"Thy friend,

"Don Quixote de la Mancha."

Sancho gave great attention to the letter; and it was highly applauded, both for sense and integrity, by everybody that heard it. After that, he rose from the table, and calling the secretary, went without any further delay and locked himself up with him in his chamber, to write an answer to his master, Don Quixote, which was as follows:—

SANCHO PANZA TO DON QUIXOTE DE LA MANCHA

"I am so taken up with business that I have not yet had time to let you know whether it goes well or ill with me in this same government, where I am more hunger-starved than when you and I wandered through woods and wildernesses.

"My lord duke wrote to me the other day to inform me of some spies that were got into this island to kill me; but as yet I have discovered none but a certain doctor, hired by the islanders to kill all the governors that come near it. They call him Dr. Pedro Rezio de Anguero, and he was born at Tirteafuera. His name is enough to make me fear he will be the death of me. This same doctor says of himself, that he does cure diseases when you have them; but when you have them not, he only pretends to keep them from coming. The physic he uses is fasting upon fasting, till he turns a body to a mere skeleton; as if to be wasted to skin and bones were not as bad as a fever. In short, he starves me to death; so that, when I thought, as being a governor, to have plenty of good hot victuals and cool liquor, and to repose on a soft feather-bed, I am come to do penance like a hermit.

"I have not yet so much as fingered the least penny of money, either for fees or anything else; and how it comes to be no better with me I cannot imagine, for I have heard that the governors who come to this island are wont to have a very good gift, or at least a very round sum given them by the town before they enter. And they say, too, that this is the usual custom, not only here but in other places.

"Last night, in going my rounds, I met with a mighty handsome damsel in boy's clothes, and a brother of hers in woman's apparel. My gentleman-waiter fell in love with the girl, and intends to make her his wife, as he says. As for the youth, I have pitched on him to be my son-in-law. To-day we both design to talk to the father, one Diego de la Llana, who is a gentleman, and an old Christian every inch of him.

"I visit the markets as you advised me, and yesterday found one of the hucksters selling hazel-nuts. She pretended they were all new; but I found she had mixed a whole bushel of old, empty, rotten nuts among the same quantity of new. With that I adjudged them to be given to the hospital boys, who know how to pick the good from the bad, and gave sentence against her that she should not come into the market for fifteen days; and people said I did well.

"I am mighty well pleased that my lady duchess has written to my wife, Teresa Pauza, and sent her the token you mention. It shall go hard but I will requite her kindness one time or other. Pray give my service to her, and tell her from me she has not cast her gift in a broken sack, as something more than words shall show.

"If I might advise you, and had my wish, there should be no falling out between your worship and my lord and lady; for, if you quarrel with them, it is I must come by the worst for it. And, since you mind me of being grateful, it will not look well in you not to be so to those who have made so much of you at their castle.

"If my wife, Teresa Panza, writes to me, pray pay the postage and send me the letter; for I have a mighty desire to know how fares it with her, and my house and children. So Heaven protect your worship from evil-minded enchanters, and bring me safe and sound out of this government; which I very much doubt, seeing how I am treated by Doctor Pedro Rezio.

"Your worship's servant,

"Sancho Panza, the Governor."

TERESA PANZA'S LETTER TO HER HUSBAND, SANCHO PANZA

"I received thy letter, dear Sancho of my soul, and I promise and swear to thee, on the faith of a Catholic Christian, I was within two finger-breadths of running mad with joy; and take notice, brother, when I heard thou wast a governor, I had liked to have dropped down dead with pure pleasure; for thou knowest they say sudden joy kills as well as deadly sorrow.

"Thy hunting-suit lay before me, the string of corals sent by lady duchess was tied round my neck, the letters were in my hand, and the messenger in my presence; and yet I imagined and believed that all I saw and handled was a dream, for who could conceive that a goatherd should come to be governor of islands? Thou knowest, my friend, that my mother said, 'One must live long to see a great deal.' This I mention because I hope to see more if I live longer, for I do not intend to stop until I see thee a farmer or collector of the revenue,— offices which, though they carry those who abuse them to the devil, are, in short, always bringing in the penny.

"My lady duchess will tell thee how desirous I am of going to court. Consider of it, and let me know thy pleasure, for I will endeavor to do thee honor there by riding in my coach.

"The curate, barber, bachelor, and even the sexton, cannot believe thou art a governor, and say the whole is a deception or matter of enchantment, like all the affairs of thy master, Don Quixote. Sampson vows he will go in quest of thee, and drive this government out of thy head, as well as the madness out of Don Quixote's skull. I say nothing, but laugh in my own sleeve, look at my beads, and contrive how to make thy hunting-suit into a gown and petticoat for our daughter. I have sent some acorns to my lady duchess, and I wish they were of gold. Send me some strings of pearls, if they are in fashion in thy island.

"The news of our town are these: the widow of the hill has matched her daughter with a bungling painter, who came here and undertook all sort of work. The corporation employed him to paint the king's arms over the gate of the town-house. He asked them two ducats for the job, which they paid beforehand; so he fell to it and worked eight days, at the end of which he had made nothing of it, and said he could not bring his hand to paint such trumpery, and returned the money; yet, for all that, he married in the name of a good workman. The truth is, he has left his brushes and taken up the spade, and goes to the field like a gentleman. Pedro de Lobo's son has taken orders and shaved his crown, meaning to be a priest. Minguilla, Mingo Silvato's niece, hearing of it, is suing him upon a promise of marriage. We have had no olives this year, nor is there a drop of vinegar to be had in all the town. A company of foot-soldiers passed through here, and carried off with them three girls. I will not say who they are; mayhap they will return, and somebody or other marry them, with all their faults. Sanchica makes bone-lace, and gets eight maravedis a day, which she drops into a saving-box, to help her toward household stuff; but now that she is a governor's daughter, she has no need to work, for thou wilt give her a portion without it. The fountain in our market-place is dried up. A thunderbolt fell upon the pillory, and there may they all alight! I expect an answer to this, and about my going to court. And so God grant thee more years than myself, or as many, for I would not willingly leave thee behind me.

"Thy wife,

"Teresa Panza."

To think that the affairs of this life are always to remain in the same state is an erroneous fancy. The face of things rather seems continually to change and roll with circular motion; summer succeeds the spring, autumn the summer, winter the autumn, and then spring again. So time proceeds in this perpetual round; only the life of man is ever hastening to its end, swifter than time itself, without hopes to be renewed, unless in the next, that is unlimited and infinite. For even by the light of nature and without that of faith, many have discovered the swiftness and instability of this present being, and the duration of the eternal life which is expected.

"I know St. Peter is well at Rome," meaning every one does well to follow the employment to which he was bred.

Let no one stretch his feet beyond the length of his sheet.

When thou art in Rome follow the fashions of Rome.

Sweet is our love of native land.

The prudent man who is expecting to be deprived of his habitation looks out for another before he is turned out of doors.

Well-got wealth may meet disaster,

But ill-got wealth destroys its master.

Bread is relief for all kind of grief.

We can bear with patience the ill-luck that comes alone.

Man projects in vain,

For God doth still ordain.

As is the reason,

Such is the season.

Let no man presume to think

Of this cup I will not drink.

Where the flitch we hope to find,

Not even a hook is left behind.

Keep a safe conscience, and let people say what they will.

It is as impracticable to tie up the tongue of malice as to erect barricades in the open fields.

"If a governor resigns his office in good circumstances, people say he must have been an oppressor and a knave; and if poverty attends him in his retreat, they set him down as an idiot and fool."

"For this time," answered Sancho, "I am certain they will think me more fool than knave."

The great Sancho Panza, the flower and mirror of all island governors.

A law neglected is the same as if it had never been enacted.

Give always to the cat

What was kept for the rat,

And let it be thy view

All mischief to eschew.

It is fitting that all who receive a benefit should show themselves grateful, though it be only a trifle.

song of altisidora.

Stay, cruel knight,

Take not thy flight,

Nor spur thy battered jade;

Thy haste restrain,

Draw in the rein,

And hear a love-sick maid.

Why dost thou fly?

No snake am I,

That poison those I love.

Gentle I am

As any lamb,

And harmless as a dove.

Thy cruel scorn

Has left forlorn

A nymph whose charms may vie

With theirs who sport

In Cynthia's court,

Though Venus' self were by.

Since, fugitive knight, to no purpose I woo thee,

Barabbas's fate still pursue and undo thee!

Like ravenous kite

That takes its flight

Soon as't has stol'n a chicken,

Thou bear'st away

My heart, thy prey,

And leav'st me here to sicken.

Three night-caps, too,

And garters blue,

That did to legs belong
Smooth to the sight
As marble white,
And faith, almost as strong.

Two thousand groans,
As many moans,
And sighs enough to fire
Old Priam's town,
And burn it down,
Did it again aspire.
Since, fugitive knight, to no purpose I woo thee,
Barabbas's fate still pursue and undo thee!
May Sancho ne'er
His buttocks bare
Fly-flap, as is his duty;
And thou still want
To disenchant
Dulcinea's injured beauty.
May still transformed,
And still deformed,
Toboso's nymph remain,
In recompense
Of thy offence,
Thy scorn and cold disdain.
When thou dost wield
Thy sword in field,
In combat, or in quarrel,
Ill-luck and harms
Attend thy arms,

Instead of fame and laurel.

Since, fugitive knight, to no purpose I woo thee,

Barabbas's fate still pursue and undo thee!

May thy disgrace

Fill every place,

Thy falsehood ne'er be hid,

But round the world

Be tossed and hurled,

From Seville to Madrid.

If, brisk and gay,

Thou sitt'st to play

At ombre or at chess,

May ne'er spadille

Attend thy will,

Nor luck thy movements bless.

Though thou with care

Thy corns dost pare,

May blood the penknife follow;

May thy gums rage,

And naught assuage

The pain of tooth that's hollow.

Since, fugitive knight, to no purpose I woo thee,

Barabbas's fate still pursue and undo thee!

Liberty is one of the most precious gifts which Heaven hath bestowed on man, exceeding all the treasures which earth encloses, or which ocean hides; and for this blessing, as well as for honor, we may and ought to venture life itself. On the other hand, captivity and restraint are the greatest evils that human nature can endure. I make this observation, Sancho, because thou hast seen the delicacies and the plenty with which we were entertained in that castle; yet, in the midst of those savory banquets and ice-cooled potations, I thought myself confined within the very straits of famine, because I did not enjoy the treat with that liberty which I should have felt had it been my own.

Obligations incurred by benefits and favors received are fetters which hamper the free-born soul.

Happy is he to whom Heaven hath sent a morsel of bread, for which he is obliged to none but Heaven itself.

The man in wisdom must be old

Who knows in giving where to hold.

All times are not the same, nor equally fortunate; and those incidents which the vulgar call omens, though not founded on any natural reason, have, even by persons of sagacity, been held and deemed as fair and fortunate. One of these superstitious omen-mongers rises in the morning, goes abroad, chances to meet a friar belonging to the beatified St. Francis; and as if he had encountered a dragon in his way, runs back to his own house with fear and consternation. Another Foresight by accident scatters the salt upon the table, by which fear and melancholy are scattered through his heart; as if Nature was obliged to foretell future misfortunes by such trivial signs and tokens; whereas a prudent man and a good Christian will not so minutely scrutinize the purposes of Heaven. Scipio, chancing to fall in landing upon the coast of Afric, and perceiving that his soldiers looked upon this accident as a bad omen, he embraced the soil with seeming eagerness, saying, "Thou shalt not 'scape me, Afric, for I have thee safe in my arms."

Love has no respect of persons, and laughs at the admonitions of reason; like Death, he pursues his game both in the stately palaces of kings and the humble huts of shepherds. When he has got a soul fairly in his clutches, his first business is to deprive it of all shame and fear.

Beauty, they say, is the chief thing in love-matters.

"Hearken to me, Sancho," said Don Quixote; "there are two kinds of beauty,—the one of the mind, the other of the body. That of the mind shines forth in good sense and good conduct, in modesty, liberality, and courtesy; and all these qualities may be found in one who has no personal attractions; and when that species of beauty captivates, it produces a vehement and superior passion. I well know, Sancho, that I am not handsome, but I know also that I am not deformed; and a man of worth, if he be not hideous, may inspire love, provided he has those qualities of the mind which I have mentioned."

Of all the sins that men commit, though some say pride, in my opinion ingratitude is the worst. It is truly said that hell is full of the ungrateful. From that foul crime I have endeavored to abstain ever since I enjoyed the use of reason; and if I cannot return the good offices done me by equal benefits, I substitute my desire to repay them; and if this be not enough, I publish them: for he who proclaims the favors he has received would return them if he could. And generally the power of the receiver is unequal to that of the giver, like the bounty of Heaven, to which no man can make an equal return. But, though utterly unable to repay the unspeakable beneficence of God, gratitude affords an humble compensation suited to our limited powers.

Lay a bridge of silver for a flying enemy.

Let Martha die, so that she be well fed.

He that has skill should handle the quill.

There is no greater folly than to give way to despair.

Patience often falls to the ground when it is over-loaded with injuries.

Alexander the Great ventured to cut the Gordian knot, on the supposition that cutting would be as effectual as untying it, and, notwithstanding this violence, became sole master of all Asia.

"Be not concerned," said Roque, addressing himself to Don Quixote, "nor tax Fortune with unkindness. By thus stumbling, you may chance to stand more firmly than ever; for Heaven, by strange and circuitous ways, incomprehensible to men, is wont to raise the fallen and enrich the needy."

Oh, maddening sting of jealousy, how deadly thy effects!

Justice must needs be a good thing, for it is necessary even among thieves.

"Signor Roque," said he, "the beginning of a cure consists in the knowledge of the distemper and in the patient's willingness to take the medicines prescribed to him by his physician. You are sick; you know your malady, and God, our physician, is ready with medicines that, in time, will certainly effect a cure. Besides, sinners of good understanding are nearer to amendment than those who are devoid of it; and, as your superior sense is manifest be of good cheer and hope for your entire recovery. If in this desirable work you would take the shortest way and at once enter that of your salvation, come with me and I will teach you to be a knight-errant,—a profession, it is true, full of labors and disasters, but which, being placed to the account of penance, will not fail to lead you to honor and felicity."

The abbot must eat that sings for his meat.

Courtesy begets courtesy.

The jest that gives pain is no jest.

That pastime should not be indulged which tends to the detriment of a fellow-creature.

The fire is discovered by its own light; so is virtue by its own excellence.

No renown equals in splendor that which is acquired by the profession of arms.

Virtue demands our homage wherever it is found.

Women are commonly impatient and inquisitive.

By a man's actions may be seen the true disposition of his mind.

"Body of me," said Don Quixote, "what a progress you have made, signor, in the Tuscan language! I would venture a good wager that where the Tuscan says piace, you say, in Castilian, plaze; and where he says piu, you say mas; and su you translate by the word arriba; and giu by abaxo."

"I do so, most certainly," quoth the author, "for such are the corresponding words."

"And yet, I dare say, sir," quoth Don Quixote, "that you are scarcely known in the world,—but it is the fate of all ingenious men. What abilities are lost, what genius obscured, and what talents despised! Nevertheless, I cannot but think that translation from one language into another, unless it be from the noblest of all languages, Greek and Latin, is like presenting the back of a piece of tapestry, where, though the figures are seen, they are obscured by innumerable knots and ends of thread, very different from the smooth and agreeable texture of the proper face of the work; and to translate easy languages of a similar construction requires no more talent than transcribing one paper from another. But I would not hence infer that translating is not a laudable exercise; for a man may be worse and more unprofitably employed. Nor can my observation apply to the two celebrated translators, Doctor Christopher de Figueroa, in his 'Pastor Fido,' and Don John de Xaurigui, in his 'Aminta,' who, with singular felicity, have made it difficult to decide which is the translation and which is the original. But tell me, signor, is this book printed at your charge, or have you sold the copyright to some bookseller?"

"I print it, sir, on my own account," answered the author, "and expect a thousand ducats by this first impression of two thousand copies. At six reals each copy they will go off in a trice."

"'Tis mighty well," quoth Don Quixote, "though I fear you know but little of the tricks of booksellers, and the juggling there is amongst them. Take my word for it, you will find a burden of two thousand volumes upon your back no trifling matter, especially if the book be deficient in sprightliness."

"What, sir!" cried the author, "would you have me give my labor to a bookseller, who, if he paid me three maravedis for it, would think it abundant, and say I was favored? No, sir, fame is not my object: of that I am already secure. Profit is what I now seek, without which fame is nothing."

"Well, Heaven prosper you, sir!" said the knight, who, passing on, observed a man correcting a sheet of a book entitled "The Light of the Soul." On seeing the title, he said, "Books of this kind, numerous as they already are, ought still to be encouraged; for numerous are the benighted sinners that require to be enlightened." He went forward, and saw another book under the corrector's hand, and, on inquiring the title, they told him it was the second part of the ingenious gentleman Don Quixote de la Mancha, written by such a one, of Tordesillas.

"I know something of that book," quoth Don Quixote, "and, on my conscience, I thought it had been burnt long before now for its stupidity; but its Martinmas will come, as it does to every hog. Works of invention are only so far good as they come near to truth and probability; as general history is valuable in proportion as it is authentic."

Rashness is not valor; doubtful hopes ought to make men resolute, not rash.

There is a remedy for all things except death.

Between said and done

A long race may be run.

He whom Heaven favors may St. Peter bless.

They that give must take.

Where there are hooks, we do not always find bacon.

Good expectation is better than bad possession.

To-day for you, and to-morrow for me.

He that falls to-day may rise to-morrow.

Great hearts should be patient under misfortunes, as well as joyful when all goes well.

I have heard say, she they call Fortune is a drunken, freakish dame, and withal so blind that she does not see what she is about; neither whom she raises, nor whom she pulls down.

One thing I must tell thee, there is no such thing in the world as fortune; nor do the events which fall out, whether good or evil, proceed from chance, but from the particular appointment of Heaven,—and hence comes the usual saying, that every man is the maker of his own fortune.

The faults of the ass should not be laid on the pack-saddle.

When it rains let the shower fall upon my cloak.

"Observe, Sancho," said Don Quixote, "there is a great deal of difference between love and gratitude. It is very possible for a gentleman not to be in love; but, strictly speaking, it is impossible he should be ungrateful."

The sin will cease when the temptation is removed.

The heart will not grieve for what the eye doth not perceive.

What prayers can ne'er gain, a leap from a hedge may obtain.

Proverbs are short maxims of human wisdom, the result of experience and observation, and are the gifts of ancient sages; yet the proverb which is not aptly applied, instead of being wisdom, is stark nonsense.

It is the part of a good servant to sympathize with his master's pains.

"Methinks," quoth Sancho, "that a man cannot be suffering much when he can turn his brain to verse-making."

SANCHO PANZA ON SLEEP

"No entiendo eso," replied Sancho; "solo entiendo que en tanto que duermo, ni tengo temor, ni esperanza, ni trabajo, ni gloria; y bien haya el que inventó el sueño, capa que cubre todos los humanos pensamientos, manjar que quita la hambre, agua que ahuyenta la sed, fuego que calienta el frio, frio que templa el ardor, y finalmente moneda general con que todas las cosas se compran, balanza y peso que iguala al pastor con el rey, y al simple con el discreto. Sola una cosa tiene mala el sueño, segun he oido decir, y es que se parece á la muerte, pues de un dormido á un muerto hay muy poca diferencia."

"I know not what that means," replied Sancho; "I only know that while I am asleep I have neither fear, nor hope, nor trouble, nor glory. Blessings light on him who first invented sleep! Sleep is the mantle that shrouds all human thoughts; the food that dispels hunger; the drink that quenches thirst; the fire that warms the cold; the cool breeze that moderates heat; in a word, the general coin that purchases every commodity; the weight and balance that makes the shepherd even with his sovereign, and the simple with the sage. There is only one bad circumstance, as I have heard, in sleep: it resembles death, inasmuch as between a dead corse and a sleeping man there is no apparent difference."

"Enjoy thy repose," said Don Quixote; "thou wast born to sleep and I to watch; and, during the little of night that remains, I will give my thoughts the rein, and cool the furnace of my reflections with a short madrigal, which I have this evening, unknown to thee, composed in my own mind."

Amor, cuando yo pienso

En el mal que me das terrible y fuerte,

Voy corriendo á la muerte,

Pensando así acabar mi mal inmenso:

Mas en llegando al paso,

Que es puerto en este mar de mi tormento,

Tanta alegría siento,

Que la vida se esfuerza, y no le paso.

Así el vivir me mata,

Que la muerte me torna á dar la vida.

O condicion no oida,

La que conmigo muerte y vida trata!

O love! when, sick of heart-felt grief,

I sigh, and drag thy cruel chain,

To death I fly, the sure relief

Of those who groan in lingering pain.

But coming to the fatal gates,

The port in this my sea of woe,

The joy I feel new life creates,

And bids my spirits brisker flow.

Thus dying every hour I live,

And living I resign my breath.

Strange power of love, that thus can give

A dying life and living death!

Till Heaven, in pity to the weeping world,

Shall give Altisidora back to day,

By Quixote's scorn to realms of Pluto hurled,

Her every charm to cruel death a prey;

While matrons throw their gorgeous robes away,

To mourn a nymph by cold disdain betrayed:

To the complaining lyre's enchanting lay

I'll sing the praises of this hapless maid,

In sweeter notes than Thracian Orpheus ever played.

Nor shall my numbers with my life expire,

Or this world's light confine the boundless song:

To thee, bright maid, in death I'll touch the lyre,

And to my soul the theme shall still belong.

When, freed from clay, the flitting ghosts among,

My spirit glides the Stygian shores around,

Though the cold hand of death has sealed my tongue,

Thy praise the infernal caverns shall rebound,

And Lethe's sluggish waves move slower to the sound.

Better kill me outright than break my back with other men's burdens.

Sleep is the best cure for waking troubles.

Devils, play or not play, win or not win, can never be content.

History that is good, faithful, and true, will survive for ages; but should it have none of these qualities, its passage will be short between the cradle and the grave.

As for dying for love, it is all a jest; your lovers, indeed, may easily say they are dying, but that they will actually give up the ghost, believe it—Judas.

"Madam," said he, "your ladyship should know that the chief cause of this good damsel's suffering is idleness, the remedy whereof is honest and constant employment. Lace, she tells me, is much worn in purgatory, and since she cannot but know how to make it, let her stick to that; for, while her fingers are assiduously employed with her bobbins, the images that now haunt her imagination will keep aloof, and leave her mind tranquil and happy. This, madam, is my opinion and advice."

"And mine, too," added Sancho, "for I never in my life heard of a lacemaker that died for love; for your damsels that bestir themselves at some honest labor think more of their work than of their sweethearts. I know it by myself; when I am digging, I never think of my Teresa, though, God bless her! I love her more than my very eyelids."

Railing among lovers is the next neighbor to forgiveness.

The ass will carry the load, but not a double load.

When money's paid before it's due,

A broken limb will straight ensue.

Delay breeds danger.

Pray to God devoutly,

And hammer away stoutly.

A sparrow in the hand is worth an eagle on the wing.

"No more proverbs, for God's sake," quoth Don Quixote, "for, methinks, Sancho, thou art losing ground, and returning to sicut erat. Speak plainly, as I have often told thee, and thou wilt find it worth a loaf per cent to thee."

"I know not how I came by this unlucky trick," replied Sancho: "I cannot bring you in three words to the purpose without a proverb, nor give you a proverb which, to my thinking, is not to the purpose;—but I will try to mend."

The straw is too hard to make pipes of.

The knight and squire ascended a little eminence, whence they discovered their village; which Sancho no sooner beheld than, kneeling down, he said: "Open thine eyes, O my beloved country! and behold thy son, Sancho Panza, returning to thee again, if not rich, yet well whipped! Open thine arms, and receive thy son Don Quixote, too! who, though worsted by another, has conquered himself, which, as I have heard say, is the best kind of victory! Money I have gotten, and though I have been soundly banged, I have come off like a gentleman."

"Leave these fooleries, Sancho," quoth Don Quixote, "and let us go directly to our homes, where we will give full scope to our imagination, and settle our intended scheme of a pastoral life."

It must here be mentioned that Sancho Panza, by way of sumpter-cloth, had thrown the buckram robe painted with flames, which he had worn on the night of Altisidora's revival, upon his ass. He likewise clapped the mitre on Dapple's head,—in short, never was an ass so honored and bedizened. The priest and bachelor, immediately recognizing their friends, ran toward them with open arms. Don Quixote alighted, and embraced them cordially. In the mean time, the boys, whose keen eyes nothing can escape, came flocking from all parts.

"Ho!" cries one, "here comes Sancho Panza's ass, as gay as a parrot, and Don Quixote's old horse, leaner than ever!"

Thus, surrounded by the children and accompanied by the priest and the bachelor, they proceeded through the village till they arrived at Don Quixote's house, where, at the door, they found the housekeeper and the niece, who had already heard of his arrival. It had likewise reached the ears of Sancho's wife, Teresa, who, half-naked, with her hair about her ears, and dragging Sanchica after her, ran to meet her husband; and seeing him not so well equipped as she thought a governor ought to be, she said: "What makes you come thus, dear husband? methinks you come afoot and foundered! This, I trow, is not as a governor should look."

"Peace, wife," quoth Sancho; "the bacon is not so easily found as the pin to hang it on. Let us go home, and there you shall hear wonders. I have got money, and honestly, too, without wronging anybody."

"Hast thou got money, good husband? Nay, then, 't is well, however it be gotten; for, well or ill, it will have brought up no new custom in the world."

All things human, especially the lives of men, are transitory, ever advancing from their beginning to their decline and final determination.

"The greatest folly," said Sancho, "that a man can commit in this world, is to give himself up to death without any good cause for it, but only from melancholy."

THE WILL OF DON QUIXOTE

"I feel, good sirs," said Don Quixote, "that death advances fast upon me. Let us then be serious, and bring me a confessor, and a notary to draw up my will, for a man in my state must not trifle with his soul. Let the notary be sent for, I beseech you, while my friend here, the priest, is taking my confession."

The priest, having listened to his dying friend's confession, came out of the room and told them that the good Alonzo Quixano was near his end, and certainly in his right senses; he therefore advised them to go in, as it was full time that his will should be made. These tidings gave a terrible stab to the overcharged hearts of the two ladies and his faithful squire, whose eyes overflowed with weeping, and whose bosoms had well-nigh burst with a thousand sighs and groans; for, indeed, it must be owned, as we have somewhere observed, that whether in the character of Alonzo Quixano the

Good, or in the capacity of Don Quixote de la Mancha, the poor gentleman had always exhibited marks of a peaceable temper and agreeable demeanor, for which he was beloved, not only by his own family, but also by all those who had the pleasure of his acquaintance.

The notary entering the apartment with the rest of the company, wrote the preamble of the will, in which Don Quixote disposed of his soul in all the necessary Christian forms; then proceeding to the legacies, he said:—

"Item: whereas, Sancho Panza, whom, in my madness, I made my squire, has in his hands a certain sum of money for my use; and, as divers accounts, disbursements, and pecuniary transactions have passed between us, it is my will that he shall not be charged or brought to account for the said money; but, if there be any overplus after he has deducted the payment of what I owe him, the said overplus, which must be a mere trifle, shall be his own, and much good may it do him; and as, during my disorder, I contributed to his being made governor of an island, I would now, while I enjoy my perfect senses, confer upon him, were it in my power, a whole kingdom, which he richly deserves for the innocency of his heart and the fidelity of his service."

Then turning to the disconsolate squire, "Forgive me, friend," said he, "for having been the cause of thy appearing in the eye of the world a madman like myself, by drawing thee into my erroneous notions concerning the existence and adventures of knights-errant."

"Gentlemen," said Don Quixote, "let us proceed fair and softly. I was mad, I am now sane; I was Don Quixote de la Mancha; I am now, as formerly styled, Alonzo Quixano the Good. And may my repentance and sincerity restore me to the esteem you once had for me. Now let the notary proceed.

"Item: I bequeath to Antonia Quixano, my niece, here present, all my estate, real and personal, after the payment of all my debts and legacies; and the first to be discharged shall be the wages due to my housekeeper for the time she has been in my service, and twenty ducats besides for a suit of mourning.

"I appoint for my executors signor the priest and signor bachelor Sampson Carrasco, here present.

"Item: It is also my will that, if Antonia Quixano, my niece, should be inclined to marry, it shall be only with a man who, upon the strictest inquiry, shall be found to know nothing of books of chivalry; and, in case it appear that he is acquainted with such books, and that my niece, notwithstanding, will and doth marry him, then shall she forfeit all I have bequeathed her, which my executors may dispose of in pious uses as they think proper.

"And, finally, I beseech the said gentlemen, my executors, that if haply they should come to the knowledge of the author of a certain history dispersed abroad, entitled, 'The Second Part of the Achievements of Don Quixote de la Mancha,' that they will, in my name, most earnestly entreat him to forgive me for having been the innocent cause of his writing such a number of absurdities as that performance contains; for I quit this life with some scruples of conscience arising from that consideration."

The will being thus concluded, he was seized with a fainting-fit, and stretched himself at full length in the bed, so that all the company were alarmed and ran to his assistance. During three days which he lived after the will was signed and sealed, he frequently fainted, and the whole family was in confusion. Nevertheless, the niece ate her victuals, the housekeeper drank to the repose of his soul, and even Sancho cherished his little carcass; for the prospect of succession either dispels or moderates that affliction which an heir ought to feel at the death of the testator.

At last Don Quixote expired, after having received all the sacraments, and in the strongest terms, pathetically enforced, expressed his abomination against all books of chivalry; and the notary observed, that in all the books of that kind which he had perused, he had never read of any knight-errant who died quietly in his bed as a good Christian, like Don Quixote; who, amidst the tears and lamentations of all present, gave up the ghost, or, in other words, departed this life. The curate was no sooner certified of his decease, than he desired the notary to make out a testimonial, declaring that Alonzo Quixano the Good, commonly called Don Quixote de la Mancha, had taken his departure from this life, and died of a natural death; that no other author, different from Cid Hamet Benengeli, should falsely pretend to raise him from the dead, and write endless histories of his achievements.

This was the end of that extraordinary gentleman of La Mancha, whose birthplace Cid Hamet was careful to conceal, that all the towns and villages of that province might contend for the honor of having produced him, as did the seven cities of Greece for the glory of giving birth to Homer. The lamentations of Sancho, the niece and the housekeeper, are not here given, nor the new epitaphs on the tomb of the deceased knight, except the following one, composed by Sampson Carrasco:—

Here lies the valiant cavalier,

Who never had a sense of fear:

So high his matchless courage rose,

He reckoned death among his vanquished foes.

Wrongs to redress, his sword he drew,

And many a caitiff giant slew;
His days of life though madness stained,
In death his sober senses he regained.

www.ingramcontent.com/pod-product-compliance
Lightning Source LLC
LaVergne TN
LVHW040058080526
838202LV00045B/3693